## PRAISE FOR *S...*

"This work is so import...

and right away I could te.. Granddaughter Crow feels the same. This is the journey to freedom. Her introduction got me ready to do more of my own work with the shadow. Granddaughter Crow not only gives you the shamanic approach for this work, but she also brings in science, psychology, history, and culture, making connections across all parts of our consciousness. *Shamanism and Your Shadow* opens your mind to the depths of this work. The journey through the shadow, with the help of the four totems, will provide you with deep reflection and a closer look at the self, leading you right into a higher state of being. *Shamanism and Your Shadow* is an excellent book to work with. The guided meditations, journal prompts, and connections to the natural world are beautiful ways to embrace your shadow side. I'm thrilled that this book is available for the individual journey through the shadow."

—**STEFANI MICHELLE**, author of *Chakras & Shadow Work*

"Granddaughter Crow guides us through understanding our shadow work by helping us find our shadows. She does this through several techniques that make up her four-stage process of shadow work. It's not your typical shadow work I've read before. It requires an understanding of elemental medicine, journaling, chants, and the courage to boldly look into ourselves for inner healing and completion of the trauma cycle. This book is a beacon for those seeking deeper spiritual understanding and personal growth. It eloquently bridges ancient traditions with contemporary relevance, making it a must-read for anyone on a path of self-discovery and healing. My great grandma would say,

'Eat the fruit and spit the seeds.' With this book, it's fruit for the soul—I can't imagine any seeds will hit your floor. Enjoy!"

—**SHERRY SHONE (AKA THAT HOODOO LADY),** author of *Hoodoo for Everyone*

# SHAMANISM
## AND YOUR
# SHADOW

## ABOUT THE AUTHOR

Granddaughter Crow (Dr. Joy Gray) holds a doctorate in leadership. Internationally recognized as a medicine woman, she comes from a long line of spiritual leaders as a member of the Navajo Nation.

She is an international award-winning author. Her books include *The Journey of the Soul*, *Wisdom of the Natural World*, and *Belief, Being, and Beyond*. In 2024, she gives respect to her lineage as she is an Honored Listee in Who's Who in America. Additionally, she is a member of the Delta Mu Delta Honor International Society in Business due to her academic achievements. She was voted Woman of the Year 2015 by the National Association of Professional Women.

She is truly a conduit for wisdom and transformation between the Western and Native worlds. More than that, she has dedicated her life to inspiring, encouraging, and empowering individuals to be their authentic selves. Visit her at www .granddaughtercrow.com.

*Granddaughter Crow* ®

# SHAMANISM

## AND YOUR

# SHADOW

Using Animal Guides to Explore and Heal Your Inner Self

# GRANDDAUGHTER CROW

LLEWELLYN
WOODBURY, MINNESOTA

FIRST EDITION
First Printing, 2025

Book design by Samantha Peterson
Cover design by Kevin R. Brown
Interior illustrations by Llewellyn Art Department
    Chakra figure on page 55 by Mary Ann Zapalac
    Vitruvian man on page 52 by Eugene Smith

Llewellyn Publications is a registered trademark of Llewellyn Worldwide Ltd.

**Library of Congress Cataloging-in-Publication Data**
Names: Granddaughter Crow, author.
Title: Shamanism and your shadow : using animal guides to explore and heal
    your inner self / by Granddaughter Crow.
Description: First edition. | Woodbury, MN : Llewellyn Publications, a
    Division of Llewellyn Worldwide Ltd., [2025] | Includes bibliographical
    references. | Summary: "Organized by the four cardinal directions and
    the animal guides associated with each one, this book provides
    everything you need to approach, recognize, understand, and accept your
    shadow"— Provided by publisher.
Identifiers: LCCN 2024045065 (print) | LCCN 2024045066 (ebook) | ISBN
    9780738779775 (paperback) | ISBN 9780738779928 (ebook)
Subjects: LCSH: Shamanism—Miscellanea. | Shadow
    (Psychoanalysis)—Miscellanea. | Animals—Miscellanea. |
    Totems—Miscellanea. | Shamans.
Classification: LCC BL2370.S5 G736 2025  (print) | LCC BL2370.S5  (ebook) |
    DDC 201/.44—dc23/eng/20241121
LC record available at https://lccn.loc.gov/2024045065
LC ebook record available at https://lccn.loc.gov/2024045066

Llewellyn Worldwide Ltd. does not participate in, endorse, or have any authority or responsibility concerning private business transactions between our authors and the public.
    All mail addressed to the author is forwarded but the publisher cannot, unless specifically instructed by the author, give out an address or phone number.
    Any internet references contained in this work are current at publication time, but the publisher cannot guarantee that a specific location will continue to be maintained. Please refer to the publisher's website for links to authors' websites and other sources.

Llewellyn Publications
A Division of Llewellyn Worldwide Ltd.
2143 Wooddale Drive
Woodbury, MN 55125-2989
www.llewellyn.com

Printed in the United States of America

## OTHER BOOKS BY GRANDDAUGHTER CROW

*Belief, Being, and Beyond*

*The Journey of the Soul*

*Wisdom of the Natural World*

I would like to dedicate this book to the best friend that I have ever had, and he is also my beloved husband: Jeffrey Gray. Without you, Jeffrey, this book would not be—you're a brilliant man. Through the inspiration, encouragement, and empowerment that you give to me, this book was written. I am grateful that you came into my life. I am honored to write this book with you. I am blessed to call you my love. You are the dark poet, and your poetry is once again shared with the rest of the world. Thank you, my beloved Jeffrey Gray! Hale and Whole!

# CONTENTS

# DISCLAIMER

The practices and techniques described in this book should not be used as an alternative to professional medical treatment. This book is not meant to provide medical diagnoses, treatments, prescriptions, or suggestions for medication in relation to any human disease, pain, injury, or condition. Please consult a certified medical practitioner to obtain a diagnosis for any physical or mental ailments you experience. Additionally, if you or someone you know is suffering from trauma, dissociation, or other mental ailments, please contact a licensed professional. This book is meant to complement and assist the journey of a shadow worker, but it is not the only path to wellness.

With this disclaimer out of the way, I welcome you to the wonderful world of shamanism.

# FOREWORD

All that exists is made of energy. This includes the shadow that so many fear.

Like many children of the 1990s, I was drawn to magic partly due to the presence and popularity of witches in pop culture. As a fledgling witch, I focused on changing all of the external aspects of myself: wearing black clothes and pentagram jewelry, getting tattoos, and developing an obsession with ravens and crows that I have kept to this day. I even carried quite the chip on my shoulder toward organized religion. I thought that if I wore my faith around me, that would be sufficient. If this had remained all that paganism and magic were for me, I'd have given them up long ago. Over the years, the trendiness I had allocated to my spirituality broke away and a real, tangible aspect was revealed. I was encouraged to dive beyond the glitz and glamour shown by Hollywood and get down to the work.

Looking back, I can see that during the time I spent focusing on the external, I was learning how to approach the shadow. Just as Granddaughter Crow talks about, my shadows wanted to be recognized. But first, I needed to learn they were there. Even after I acknowledged its existence, it took me years to learn to stop running from my shadows, and several more to understand that they were there to benefit me. That was my path. I needed that time.

Some of you will move more quickly into and through shadow work, and some of you will move slowly. It is not a race. Working with the shadow is perhaps the most difficult yet rewarding set of experiences a person can have in their life. It is often painful and brings us down to earth. It is also uplifting, revealing, and healing. As Granddaughter Crow reminds us, the healing lies within the pain. This is a statement that, uncomfortable as it may be to hear, is universally true. No one ever healed from a painful past by pretending it didn't exist. When working with the shadow, it is preferable to be thorough, to visit and revisit the work all the while understanding that there is no medal at the end, no gold star of completion. The rewards for shadow work are so vast and so nuanced that measuring them in tangible ways would be futile.

There is no reason to fret, however. This type of work— shadow work—is sacred. When you walk on a magical path (be it shamanism, paganism, Wicca, witchcraft, or any other), you will eventually be led to a place where you are ready for the work within this book. It could be now. It could be in decades. It could be anytime in between. If you have picked up this book and opened the pages, it may be a sign that you are ready to undergo this sacred work.

When I first met Granddaughter Crow, it was at a metaphysical event. I had just reached a point on my journey that would have put me, as I now understand it, shifting from the medicine of the owl to that of the wolf. I remember two things about her most vividly: the hat she wore and the resonance of her spirit. Crow's presence was unmistakable, joyful, and complete. I knew, before any words were spoken, that she held great healing power.

She has now chosen to share her wisdom in this book, this beautiful, imaginative book. She has chosen to help you—me—us—use the tools of a shaman to get back to a state of sacredness within our physical, mental, spiritual, and emotional selves.

She begins like all things should begin: by providing a history, which allows us to understand what shamanism is and how it can be used. Once we know that, we move forward and begin to learn what the shadow is, why it exists, and why we should not fear it. With this foundational groundwork laid, we can move forward with respect, with bravery, with humility, and armed with knowledge.

Granddaughter Crow moves you step-by-step through the shadow, using animal totems as guides. She begins with the raven, which symbolizes the death of the old self. This is preparation and acknowledgment. It is a first glimpse of sunlight, for as Crow reminds us, there is no shadow without light to cast it. She moves us to the next stage, that of the snake, where we look at societal expectations and the role shame plays in our healing journey. Then the owl, the wise bird who teaches us to see. Finally, we arrive at the wolf, where we learn to respect the knowledge the shadow provides. At each stage we are given an ingress, a way to commune with the energy of this totem.

As Crow takes us through the process of shadow work, she reminds us that emotions are necessary. Even anger, with all the stigma it carries, has a place in our world. It only becomes dangerous when it is repressed, wrongly expressed, or denied. This is a lesson I hope everyone can learn.

In her conclusion, Crow reminds us that working with the shadow is not a one-off experience. The shadows we need to see, the lessons we need to learn, they will come when the time is right. Self-healing is a lifelong pursuit. In my lifetime, I have been a student and teacher. I have been healed and been the healer. I have lived completely surrounded by my shadows and now, though they exist, they are not all I see. And still, I have more to learn, more to heal, more to discover.

Life is interesting and unexpected. Decades ago, I was so consumed by my shadows, so terrified of facing them, that I was rushing toward destruction. When I was forced to slow down and come to an inevitable stop, I had to face them. Once I did, my shadows stopped being so terrifying. All these years later, I walk with my shadows. I greet them as teachers, as allies, as sometimes friends. It has been my pleasure to read this work and an honor to write the foreword for it.

There are some books about magic. There are some books about spells. And there are some books, like this one, that are guides for healing. May you heal well.

—Awyn Dawn,
Author of *111 Magic*

# INTRODUCTION

As taboo as the shadow is, it holds so many truths. If you have light within you, you have a shadow—for only where light touches, a shadow is cast. If you are afraid of your shadow, or if you are encountering your shadow, or if you would like to discover and work with your shadow, this book is for you. This is not a book that will shame you—it is a book that will liberate you. Empower you.

## WHAT IS A SHADOW?

There are many definitions of the shadow side within us, from a psychological perspective by Carl Jung to a straightforward perspective of it being the darkness within us. Hence, it is not necessarily a concrete topic.

My personal definition is the shadow as an organic aspect of the self that is just as natural as the night is to the day.

Although one might experience the shadow side as something that is wrong, or the untamed, primal side of themselves that they wish to hide, deny, or ignore, we all have a shadow side. Approaching the shadow as an organic part of self allows one to be able to recognize, acknowledge, understand, and even respect the shadow.

When viewing the shadow as it reveals itself within the natural world, one can see that where there is light, a shadow is cast. This is not only the case for the day and the night, but also for a tree standing in the sunlight and casting a shadow underneath it; this is natural. Approaching the shadow as a natural part of oneself releases any shame or blame, and it places one in a position to work with the shadow side.

## WHAT IS A SHADOW WORKER?

A shadow worker is an individual who is able to productively work with the shadow to embrace the aspects of self that might be suppressed or hidden within the unconscious mind. Initially, it takes courage to be able to uncover and explore the shadow aspects of oneself; however, with this courage one can begin to comprehend these hidden aspects and, ultimately, respect them.

In order to become a shadow worker, an individual must be able to recognize their own shadow and where it may come from. Ultimately, they must embrace the shadow side and gain more self-knowledge in the process. This book is a guide to becoming your own shadow worker, and potentially to becoming a support system for others who are doing their personal shadow work.

No one can do shadow work for another; it is an individual process. In working with my shadow, I have learned to respect and embrace my shadow side to the point that I am a support system for others who are working with their own shadow side.

Doing shadow work is not a one-time event. Over the years, I have continued to work with my shadow side. Shadow work can be like peeling an onion—there is always another level underneath! As I have worked with each level, I have become more self-aware. Being a shadow worker is very rewarding in that it promotes self-understanding and self-care.

## WHAT IS A SHAMAN?

A shaman is an individual with a practice who interacts with the spirit world to promote balance within themselves and for others in the physical world. Although there are many different types of shamanism, as it is a global practice, there are some key aspects that most shamans have in common:

- An understanding of the sacred aspects of life and the natural world.
- The ability to effect change through trancework, be it healing, divination, or balancing energy.
- Knowledge of the unseen worlds, such as the upper world, the middle world, and the lower world. (If this is a new concept for you, imagine a tree. The upper world would be the higher branches, or higher consciousness, that you need to stretch to touch. The middle world would be the trunk of the tree, easy to touch in the three-dimensional

space you live in. The lower world would be the roots of the tree: your personal roots, and where you come from.)

There are many types of shamans. Some are traditional medicine people within a community who learn their practice from their elders. Shamans may work with the natural world that their tribe or clan comes from. There are also neoshamans, individuals who move outside of their own culture and learn shamanic practices from many different sources rather than traditional ancestral teachings. Most shamans work with plants, animals, landscapes, etc., learning from the natural world in order to understand how people can live a balanced life within themselves and within their community. In this definition, shamanism is a healing process led by the natural world.

To be clear, one does not need to be a shaman in order to work through this book. This book is to provide you with a guide to do shadow work from my shamanic perspective.

## A LITTLE BIT ABOUT ME

My name is Granddaughter Crow. This name pays homage to my Navajo ancestry and my spirit totem. I am also known as Dr. Joy Gray; I have my doctorate in leadership. I am a member of the Navajo Nation and come from a long line of spiritual leaders and medicine people (also known as shamans). My father was a full-blooded Navajo, with English being his second language. As well as being a spiritual leader, my father assisted in translating text from the English language to the Navajo language. Here is some wisdom that he shared with me:

The language of any culture is a direct reflection of the cognitive worldview of that culture. The English language speaks in terms of labels or naming things, segregating, and separating things in order to break them down into smaller parts to understand each part and the whole. If you were to ask an English speaker to "get to know a tree," they would begin to segregate and separate the parts and then name them in order to understand the tree. For example: "The tree has roots, a trunk, branches, and leaves." This is very scientifically based and works well some of the time. However, there is another way of getting to know the tree.

The Navajo language describes things and sees things as a part of the whole. One can only know a tree when one experiences a connection to the tree. Hence, in order to get to know a tree, an individual would have to stand before the tree and notice the complete organism. Next, they might notice that the leaves of the tree are moving in one gentle direction; then, they would notice their own hair is moving in the same direction. At this point, they would connect with the tree and recognize that there is something, a force, that is moving them and the tree in the same direction. They become connected to the tree and know the tree.

I have a scholarly, English-speaking mindset. Yet, I hold the natural wisdom from the Navajo mindset and bloodline. I will bridge both of these understandings in this book. I am an author and a teacher, and I have worked with individuals from this unique perspective for decades. I am excited to share this wisdom with you.

## WHAT YOU WILL FIND IN THIS BOOK

In this book, I will help you journey into the lands that may be undiscovered within you, lands that you will likely find familiar. This book is for your personal journey of self-discovery to connect to the organic yet solitary shaman that lies within you, the aspect of yourself that can connect with the natural world and learn from the wisdom of Mother Nature to balance or rebalance your energy and the light and the shadow that dwell within each of us. You will be guided to establish yourself as a shadow worker in your own regard. This is a book of truth, and a book that will lead you to more of your personal truth.

The main point of this book is to assist you in finding and working with your shadow self. Reaching the end of this book is a rite of passage. Once you are able to complete the work, then and only then will you be able to walk with another as they begin their own shadow work. Shadow work is a magical practice so raw and powerful that some choose not to partake in it. However, if the shadow is considered in the same way it appears in the natural world, maybe you will have the courage to meet it and, in turn, find more totality within yourself, as well as a wellspring of creativity and empowerment.

I am not afraid of your truth, for I have found my own truth. I am not afraid of your shame, for I have found my own shame. I am not afraid of your ugliness, nor your beauty, for I understand and embrace my own. I found more of myself—my complete self—once I was able to face my personal shadow. I am not afraid of the shadow, for I am befriending the shadow within me. As such, I embrace you and your shadow—I embrace all of you. And because of this, I understand the journey of self-discovery, self-knowledge, and self-respect. I have ventured into uncharted territory: that which is not spoken of, and that which is hidden. I have touched the silhouette of who I am, where I come from, and who I am granting myself the courage to become. May this book do the same for you.

## HOW THIS BOOK WORKS: AN OVERVIEW

This book is divided into two parts. Part I is dedicated to understanding the shadow. It explores the shadow from different perspectives, the biology of the shadow, where the shadow may come from, and clearer definitions of the terms *shamanism* and *shaman*. Part II of the book is dedicated to meeting the shadow—here is where the actual work begins.

In part II, you will find a fourfold process: (1) recognize, (2) acknowledge, (3) understand, and (4) respect your shadow. This process holds a lot of information and instruction. Hence, I recommend taking your time performing these exercises. Leave a few days, a week, or longer between each of the four stages. Move at your own pace and take your time.

One chapter is devoted to each stage of the process. In these chapters, you will find specific animal guides, guided meditations, and journal prompts. Please take all the time that you need with these exercises in order to get the most out of them. If you choose to postpone the exercises until you finish the book, that is absolutely fine. You get to decide how you wish to work your magic. Even after you have completed each of the exercises, you can certainly pick up the book next year and do them again. These exercises are designed to meet you wherever you are in life.

The final part of each chapter is packed with interpretations of the key elements within the exercise, including the meaning of the spirit animal; the time of day, season, landscape, and direction on the medicine wheel that are aligned with the chapter; how to work with the tool that is provided; and more. This information is provided for ease of access; however, feel free to explore interpretations from other trusted sources in order to get the most out of your work, especially when it comes to what you experienced during your guided meditations.

Each of the four stages works alongside you as you begin your shadow work journey. Each stage asks you to find the beauty that lies within you without fear or shame. The more you find yourself and your truth, the more you can see others and their truths. The process of experiencing life with courage, grace, and respect will assist you in seeing the world with courage, grace, and respect.

# PART I
# UNDERSTANDING THE SHADOW

# 1

# THE SHADOW

There are many definitions of the shadow side that lives within all of us. Basically, the shadow is the hidden aspect of ourselves that doesn't line up with our ideal persona. For example, the shadow may express itself as defensiveness, attacking others, or even despondency—any expressions that one might regret or feel ashamed of later, once they are out of the situation. The shadow is the part of ourselves that we would like to hide, deny, or ignore. However, through shadow work, we can begin to come to terms with these aspects of self as we move them from the darkness of the unconscious mind to the light of the conscious mind.

The shadow is alive! Life wants to be recognized. Life wants to be acknowledged, to be understood, to be respected. How can this happen if the shadow isn't recognized and acknowledged, understood, and respected?

If I see my shadow as bad and/or shameful, it will hide from me. If it hides from me or if I hide from it, the shadow will exist in a primitive state. The poet Kahlil Gibran stated that we have a "god-self" and a "primitive-self," and as a human, we stand in the twilight with both sides within us: "And you who would understand justice, how shall you unless you look upon all deeds in the fullness of light? Only then shall you know that the erect and the fallen are but one man standing in twilight between the night of his pygmy-self and the day of his god-self."[1]

Everyone has a shadow. If one denies that they have a shadow, it can lead to tragedy. You see, if you run away from your shadow, it will still exist. If you hide from your shadow, or if your shadow hides from you, you do not gain the fullness of self-awareness— and you are less complete in your knowledge of self. This book has been written for you to learn how to work with your own shadow. Then, this book becomes a reference that you can consult if you choose to help others as a shadow worker.

If you are holding this book in your hands, if you are reading these pages, you are truly a soul that seeks to understand more of yourself and others. If you are engaged thus far, you carry within you the courage to explore what else is out there—and what more is within you. If you have reached this point, I believe that your shadow is seeking you just as much as you are seeking your shadow.

## THE PSYCHOLOGY OF THE SHADOW

Carl Jung, a psychoanalyst, coined the phrase *shadow self* to refer to the hidden and potentially less-civilized aspects of the self. Let's examine the shadow from the position of psychology.

1. Gibran, *The Prophet*, chap. 12.

## Freud's Definition

Sigmund Freud is considered the father of psychology. Freud developed the concept of the three main parts of our psyche: the id, the ego, and the superego. He thought that these three aspects of the self were the structures that governed the personality and motivation of every human being.

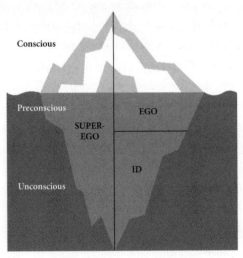

The id, ego, and superego

According to Freud, the id is fully unconscious. This means that the id affects personality in a way that the individual is not aware of. The id demands immediate gratification; it is pleasure seeking. The id wants to avoid pain and to alleviate any form of tension; this is what Freud referred to as the *pleasure principle*.

The superego is mostly—but not completely—unconscious, as can be seen in the figure above. The superego is the aspect of personality that takes the moral high road. It is driven by wanting to do things for others and seeks the ideal outcome. It is described as the moralistic part of the mind; it is the conscience. The superego wants to believe that we never think, feel, or do anything morally wrong. This is what Freud referred to as the *moral principle*. Understandably, the superego can create an immense amount of guilt and shame if confronted with the fact that we did not think, feel, or behave in a morally "correct" manner.

The ego is the most conscious aspect of the psyche. The ego acts as an intermediary between the personality aspects of the id and the superego, and it will do its best to balance any divisions within the psyche. Because the ego is referred to as the conscious part of the self, it is the aspect of personality that we perceive to be our truest self. Freud referred to this as the *reality principle*. Although the ego is deemed the organized and realistic side of self, it also has the ability to unknowingly distort reality.

These concepts will assist us in examining and explaining how the human psyche works.

## Jung's Approach

As Freud was beginning to make a name for himself within the psychological community, Carl Jung was still in his adolescent years. By the time that Freud was widely recognized, Jung had finally become a published author. They began to dialogue with each other.

Freud and Jung didn't always see eye-to-eye, including the way that each of them viewed the unconscious part of the mind. Jung believed that Freud saw the unconscious part of the mind as a depository for unwanted emotions and repressed desires that were viewed as unacceptable by the individual. Hence, everything that an individual wanted to ignore about their personality went into the unconscious mind. However, Jung believed that the unconscious was more than that—he viewed it as more of a storehouse of memories from both the individual and their ancestral history. Jung didn't view the unconscious as wanted or unwanted, good or bad.

Freud and Jung had multiple conversations about their views and still held two very different positions on the functions of the unconscious mind; they belonged to two different schools of thought. Together, their work allows us to examine a more extensive perspective of the conscious and unconscious aspects of the mind. This provides the psychology community with a broader knowledge base.

Jung was the one who coined the phrase *the shadow self*. He often referred to the shadow in his work. According to Jung, the shadow self is the dark side of our unconscious mind, and everyone has this shadow aspect. Initially, most individuals have a hard time recognizing their shadow, let alone facing it without the assistance of another. The shadow is known to store the inferior characteristics of the psyche, characteristics that are not socially acceptable to others or even to the conscious self. Admitting what we are truly capable of is difficult.

Jung believed that the shadow side was not something to be defeated, but rather something to be understood. If tamed, he believed the shadow could lead to personal cultivation and the evolution of the mind. In other words, one could find enlightenment by bringing the shadow into the light of consciousness. Instead of destroying the id, as Freud would posture, Jung believed it could be dissolved and integrated.

The shadow, by nature, stays hidden from the self so that each of us may continue to believe, with conviction, that we are good and moral human beings. It hides so that we can fit in socially. However, if the shadow self is repressed, it will seep out in disturbing ways.

### *Morality*

What constitutes a "good" and "moral" human being? From a philosophical position, morality is a set of rules and/or conventions that instruct us to cooperate with each other in an "appropriate" way. If these conventions are normalized or assumed to be the "only" way of behaving, why are there so many different moral codes found around the world? The short answer is that cultures differ across the globe, and as such, moral codes differ. Morals and moral codes need to be an agreed-upon standard within a group or society, and they should not be created by anyone outside the group. This way, the collective functions with the equal expression of all.

Moral codes change depending on the day and age. Hence, what was once considered immoral may now be seen as moral, and what was once considered moral may now be seen as immoral. Moral codes need to be reexamined and adjusted over time. This way, people are setting standards that are most beneficial for the functionality of the current collective society.

Most children will adhere to and adopt the moral code that was taught to them. As we age, many of us reexamine our morals. However, some people do not. There are those who will not question their morals even if the times and the people around them have changed or evolved, or even if their moral code no longer makes sense to them. If this continues for generations, it leads to an oversimplified understanding of life and of morality. An oversimplified understanding of morality can stop us from tapping into the deeper recesses of our psyche. Even the moral judgments of what is acceptable and what is not acceptable (good and bad) need to be questioned so that we don't uphold a moral code that limits ourselves and those around us.

Friedrich Nietzsche was a nineteenth-century German philosopher whose work challenged long-standing beliefs and belief systems. He did this by questioning and breaking down what different populations considered to be "universal truths." Nietzsche then created "moral codes" from these truths. By questioning ideologies, he discovered a deeper sense of what it means to be a human being: our truths and our morals.

Nietzsche also warned of the dangers of not reexamining our moral code. This would create "a smaller, almost ridiculous type, a herd animal, something eager to please, sickly, and mediocre"[2] — in other words, "sheeple." Nietzsche not only gave us permission to examine our moral code, he demanded it.

So, why do people avoid examining their moral code? What are we so afraid of? Maybe we are afraid of change, or maybe we are worried that we will begin to accept something we used to think was unacceptable. At any rate, it is difficult to accept aspects of ourselves that we thought were undesirable. However, if we continue to ignore ourselves—including the parts of self that we are frightened of—we will certainly ignore the reality around us. On the contrary, if we examine these aspects, we can experience liberation, as we no longer have to hide parts of ourselves.

2. Nietzsche, *Beyond Good & Evil*, chap. 5.

### *Integrating the Shadow*

Jung's approach to the shadow self invites us to explore the shadow and bring it out of the darkness and into the light. Becoming aware of the shadow is the first step to integrate the shadow into consciousness, which allows us to become more complete. Although the shadow may contain disturbing impulses, it also contains creativity and amazing capabilities. The shadow, once realized, brings a sense of renewal and deeper understanding. We can create more positive impulses with this integrated energy.

 ## JUDGMENT AND FORGIVENESS

I would like to briefly approach the concepts of judgment and forgiveness. Although we can examine the concepts of judgment and forgiveness within life, the more frightening concept is often judgment and forgiveness once we die. Many belief systems tell us that we will meet our judge and jury when we pass on. Some belief systems suggest that if we don't live a good life or ask for forgiveness for our wrongdoings, we will go to a place called hell, where we will suffer in pain forever. Other belief systems state that we will reincarnate into another form and continue to learn lessons and evolve until we reach a state of enlightenment. Still other belief systems tell us that there are a series of tests that we must pass if we want to go to a peaceful place. However, each belief system agrees that if you live a good life, you will become immortal or continue to a heavenly afterlife. I find this concept interesting; let's examine it for a moment.

## Cultural Examinations

In the Egyptian belief system, the deceased stood before Anubis, the god of the dead, or the god of passage into the underworld. At this point they entered the underworld and faced all that they had become, and they also faced the rawness of their souls and actions. There were many different tests to pass within the underworld, including encountering different monstrous beings who asked questions to test the deceased's knowledge of the underworld. If they could traverse this section, they moved into Ma'at's hall.

Ma'at was the Egyptian goddess of truth and justice. In Ma'at's hall, the deceased met forty-two assessor gods who had to be convinced that they were just and pure. As they moved through this process, the idea was that the deceased's heart would not betray them as they stood in judgment.

At this point, Anubis weighed the deceased's heart against a feather on a scale. The human heart was seen as the seat of emotion, memory, and intelligence, and the feather represented divine order. Hence, the heart was set on one side of the scale and a feather on the other to see if the individual's emotions, memory, and intelligence were in balance with divine order. Anything that an individual had done within their life that did not align with or balance with divine order made the heart heavier. If the heart was heavier than the feather, it was eaten by Ammit, a name that means "the devourer." Ammit was part crocodile, part lion, and part hippopotamus. If Ammit ate the heart, that was the end for the deceased—they would not have an afterlife. On the other hand, if the deceased's heart was as light as a feather, they had successfully completed this rite of passage and could continue to the afterlife. The afterlife was a pleasant experience, and the deceased could dwell in this heavenly place for eternity.

The Greeks believed that the deceased was met by the ferryman of the underworld, Charon, and the river Styx. The river Styx was the body of water that separated the earth and the underworld, what some might refer to as life and death. The ferryman's job was to take the souls of the deceased from the middle world to the underworld, or in other words, from the land of the living to the land of the dead. This was not free—there was a price. When a loved one died, family members could place a coin with their body, either in their mouth or over their eyes. This coin was how the deceased would pay the ferryman to allow passage. For those who died without this coin, they could not pay the ferryman, and they wouldn't be allowed into the afterlife. Their fate was to roam the river Styx for eternity. However, if the deceased could pay the ferryman's price, he would transport them to the land of the dead. Again, there was a test/judge/price to be paid during the great transition from life to death.

There are many more examples of belief systems that tell us that each of us will face a form of judgment or a test at the end of life. They agree that someone will hold us accountable for our actions. As I reflected on these belief systems, I asked myself, *Who is this being that we stand before?*

## My Take on the Matter

What if I am my own judge at the end of my lifetime? I am the hardest on myself. I judge myself and hold myself accountable for things that I would easily forgive others for. Forgiving myself is the most difficult thing for me to do. I have been harder on myself, with less forgiveness for myself, than I have ever been on another human being. Wouldn't it make sense if my own soul stood before me at the end of my life? After all, I am the one who knows what I have done and why. I understand my motives, my reasons, and my mistakes too. It would stand to reason that the only judge qualified to judge my life is me.

It is easier to forgive someone's actions when I forgive myself for my actions; forgiving myself helps me to forgive others, and forgiving others helps me to forgive myself. This concept applies to shadow work: If I can seek to understand my shadow—the aspects of myself that I hide from myself—then I can seek to understand others' shadow sides too. I am the hardest on myself, yet if I can forgive myself, I have embraced my humanity. Seek to understand the shadow—it allows the soul to be free.

## THE NATURAL WORLD

Another way to conceptualize the shadow is by looking at the rules that nature follows. This can also be called *universal law*, or the laws of the Universe, cosmos, and the natural world. This is separate from manmade law: Manmade law is when a group of individuals create laws and guidelines for others in order to keep peace and balance within that community. These laws and guidelines change over time and vary depending on location. For example, there are manmade laws about what side of the road to drive on. In short, manmade law can change, but natural law remains the same throughout space and time.

Natural law is created by nature itself and cannot be changed. There are a set of laws in place that create order within the Universe, such as the law of cause and effect, gravitational pull, and the sun always rising in the east. Here is an example of one natural law, the Law of Duality: "Any concept or force may be divided into two totally opposite concepts or forces, each of which contains the essence of the other. Opposites can be defined only in relation to each other."[3] When I peer into nature, I see many dualities. Nature shows us light and dark, day and night, height and depth, cold and hot, etc. This is not to be confused with good and evil—good and evil are not dualities; they are manmade concepts that allow us to create a moral code so that we may function as a society. Natural laws can be found in nature. Nature doesn't say that something is good and something else is evil. Yes, creatures get hurt and die in nature, but it is mankind that assigns meaning to it. Stating that something is good or bad is a human idea, whereas nature simply *is*.

What if we looked to the natural world and saw the shadow from that point of view? It would shift our perspective from looking at the shadow as "bad" or "evil" in the same way that we do not see light as inherently good or right. It would allow us to look at the shadow for what it is. Consider the shadow of a tree.

3. Whitcomb, *Magician's Companion*, 15.

I enjoy having a picnic, reading a book, and meditating under the shadow of a tree. From this perspective, I recognize that everything that is in the light casts a shadow at one point or another. You see, the shadow is natural, as natural as light.

# 2

# THE BIOLOGY OF THE SHADOW

As I reflected on the shadow, I became curious about where it came from. I have a theory. I believe that some of the shadow comes from DNA. It stands to reason that if I can inherit some of my ancestor's gifts and talents, I may inherit some of their shadows as well. In addition, I believe some of the shadow comes from repressing authentic parts of ourselves because of societal norms or the moral standards of the community we were born into. Remember, Nietzsche believed the danger of all dangers was not examining our individual and societal moral codes.

I believe the shadow is tainted by other people's projections of what is acceptable and what is not acceptable. I may be fine with parts of my shadow when I am in the privacy of my own home, but I may hide these aspects of myself in public or in certain settings. Yes, we must use discretion, but I am not speaking about discretion here—I am speaking about shame. If you feel ashamed of who you are, this can become part of your shadow as well. Clearly, shame is something that is projected onto another; it is not organic. Shaming is a sword that many groups wield in order to control their members. Shaming can also cause an individual to reject innate aspects of themselves in order to please those around them and feel a sense of belonging.

At times, I have projected my shadow self onto another person. In those moments, I was not aware that this was what I was doing. Things that I did not want to face within myself led to my judgments of others. My accusations were my confessions. Make sure that you are not casting your shadow onto another. Instead, challenge yourself to embrace it.

## TRAUMA, DISSOCIATION, AND TRIGGERS

What if the shadow was a defense mechanism created by the most primal side of self, the survival instinct? When a phenomenon occurs that is perceived to be life-threatening—whether this is a significant traumatic experience or an accumulation of smaller traumas over time—the body has a chemical reaction to provide us with a coping mechanism. However, this chemical reaction also leads to a breakdown in fundamental functionality and behavior, which can cause us to be more reactive than proactive. I have a theory that parts of the shadow are created due to traumatic experiences. If parts of the shadow developed as a defense mechanism due to a traumatic event, it makes sense that the shadow would get triggered by little things. In its own way, the shadow side is simply trying to defend us from being retraumatized.

At this point, I would like to let you know that I am certified in trauma resolution through somatic experience. I took a course that was taught by a neuroscientist and a Brazilian shaman who was also a licensed therapist. These two teachers taught me about trauma resolution from a neuroscience perspective and a shamanic perspective; it was an amazing class. With that being said, I am not a licensed therapist. As you read, please take care of yourself, and if you are confronted with traumatic memories, consider seeking professional help. I have shared my understandings, knowledge, and experiences in this chapter, and my story may bring up uncomfortable thoughts and feelings for you. If you find yourself in a position where self-care is needed, please do what is right for you.

Although it is unfortunate, stressors, traumas, and anxieties are a part of life for all creatures. Life is hard, not because you did something wrong or are being punished, but because that is just life. As you work to understand your shadow, you will begin to clear away any residual energy or debris that may have been projected onto it. Additionally, you will clear away any assumptions that you have made about your shadow. At this point, you may not completely understand your shadow, but you are acknowledging its existence.

## The Trauma Cycle

The trauma cycle is an organic process that is instilled within each of us. I know the word *trauma* can set off alarm bells and red flags, but I am here to explain that it is natural, and it has a natural cycle to it. All human beings have a primal subconsciousness that overrides the conscious mind: the amygdala. The amygdala gets activated when the body senses that it is in a life-threatening situation. This happens so quickly that it is not an idea or a thought; it is a sense that cannot be controlled. The amygdala then activates a fight, flight, or freeze response. When this happens, the conscious mind escapes the body so that it will not feel the impact of said threat. The conscious mind returns when the body senses that it is in a safe environment. Safety is key here; once the body senses that it is in a safe environment, only then will all of our mental faculties return, and only at this point is the individual able to reconnect with their body.

Here is a more detailed explanation of the trauma cycle:

1. We are confronted with a traumatic event or situation. A traumatic event is any event that signals to the body that there is a life-threatening interference. Whether that interference is physical, emotional, mental, or spiritual, there is a threat.

2. The amygdala, now activated, initiates an immediate response (typically a fight, flight, or freeze response). This response is so powerful that it overrides any conscious thought processes.

3. When the amygdala is activated, the conscious mind exits the situation. This is called dissociation. We disassociate for our protection—for our survival. This is a natural response to a traumatic event.

4. People have different responses to traumatic events. **For those of us whose instinctive response is to freeze, we**

may dissociate and lie dormant until our system perceives a safe environment. This dissociation or dormancy has no time limit to it. It can last for a lifetime—or what seems to be a lifetime. Only once the nervous system perceives safety can we complete the cycle. **For those of us whose instinctive response is to fight**, we will continue to take action, even if these actions don't make sense to the outside world. In this way, we are seeking safety by any means necessary. **For those of us whose instinctive response is to flee**, we will take action by leaving the situation to find a place of safety. In short, we may respond to traumatic events differently; however, finding a place of safety is the goal.

5. Eventually, we perceive a safe environment. There is a moment of peace, a feeling of safety, or an event that brings a sense of "I am okay." Then, the body surges with an adrenaline rush so we can fully exit the dangerous situation.

6. With this adrenaline rush, we are able to run to safety. We are given this adrenaline rush as a natural flow in order to get out of the way of the life-threatening situation.

7. Once we use this adrenaline rush to run to safety, the amygdala calms down and consciousness moves back into the body, and the nervous system becomes regulated once again.

What happens when we don't complete this natural cycle? What happens if the cycle is interrupted? First, let's examine the most likely reason this natural cycle is interrupted.

For the most part, this cycle is interrupted in steps six and seven. It is only at the end of the trauma cycle that we can begin to process what we just experienced. A final adrenaline rush cools down the amygdala. For many, this adrenaline-filled processing manifests as shaking or crying. In today's day and age, people tend to respond to this with very unaware rhetoric like "Why are you breaking down and crying now? The danger has passed. What is wrong with you?" There are often feelings of shame or embarrassment attached to the trembles of adrenaline, even though these trembles are working to cool the amygdala and complete the cycle.

In traditional Native ways, we understood that trembling or crying after a traumatic incident meant an individual was letting down their guard so they could begin to process and feel the sensations of what had happened within a safe environment. The shaman and tribe members would be expecting the adrenaline rush to kick in and recognized it for what it was. They came forward with drums and rattles to stir up this energy, acknowledge it, respect it, and release the energy from the individual.

While the medical community now recognizes that an adrenaline response can be connected to trauma, many people still see it as a "delayed reaction" or even as an "overdramatization" of a lived experience. This can place pressure on an individual to interrupt the final stage of the trauma cycle by holding in their reaction or trying to explain their "delayed" reaction. Unfortunately, there are not enough support mechanisms in place to help people understand this part of the trauma cycle.

## Triggers Are Instilled

When the trauma cycle is interrupted, the nervous system cannot reset itself properly. A trigger is subconsciously instilled to warn the individual of future situations that may lead to the same type of trauma. Triggers are a safety mechanism.

Anything can be a trigger. Triggers are usually connected to one of the five senses. The five senses help us recognize the world around us and guide us toward food, shelter, and safety. The five senses are also able to detect danger and potentially traumatic or life-threating situations. Therefore, a trigger could be anything from the voice of an abuser to the color of the hat an abuser was wearing at the time of the trauma.

Triggers are in place to keep us out of harm's way. However, they do this by reminding us of a previous trauma, which could potentially start the cycle all over again, immediately causing the nervous system to become dysregulated. When trauma has been healed, the body may avoid similar situations if a trigger is still in place. However, at that point, the trigger does not cause such a strong reaction. It is more of a sense of knowing that a situation is potentially unsafe.

Being triggered often leads to one of three outcomes:

- The trauma has not completed its cycle, so the trigger response is as though the past situation is going on in the present. The individual gets thrown back, mentally and emotionally, to the original trauma and responds accordingly.

- The trauma has completed its cycle, but the trigger is still intact. The memory of the traumatic situation arises, but the individual has an understanding that it was in the past and does not dissociate. However, the individual may need time to digest this.

- The trauma cycle has been completed, and the trigger is disassembled (i.e., no longer intact). This is the hope for everyone who has experienced and encountered trauma.

## Dissociation

Dissociation is a common part of the trauma cycle, but it is often misunderstood. Simply put, dissociation is when consciousness disconnects from the physical body and the current situation. This is a way for our consciousness to avoid, distract, or numb us from a situation that we are not able to fully digest. Dissociation does not always occur during the trauma cycle; sometimes it happens when we hear life-changing news or are driving from one location to another. All of this is normal. However, in this book we are focusing on dissociation as a response to a traumatic experience or a trigger that was installed from a traumatic event.

Dissociation is the mind's way of protecting itself—and us—from reliving an experience that we are not able to cope with at the present time. This may be experienced as a time lapse or a memory lapse. Of course, memory lapses are common and are part of aging; that is not the same thing as dissociation. Most likely, dissociation is a result of physical trauma or psychological trauma. It doesn't need to be quantified on a scale or compared to another's experience; it is unique to an individual's lived experience. Some individuals have experienced situations that cause them to dissociate more quickly in order to protect the mind.

Dissociation also occurs during moments in life when we cannot understand or digest what is happening; we may attempt to push everything to the back of the mind. When life becomes overwhelming, our natural release valve kicks in, and we begin to dissociate. This is a normal coping mechanism that many individuals experience.

Dissociation can be mild or severe. Mild dissociation is more common than you might think. If you are experiencing severe dissociation, please seek medical attention; if you are working with someone who is experiencing severe dissociation, recognize it and find a trained professional who can support them. If an individual's personality is quickly changing, that can be an indication that they are experiencing severe dissociation and will require additional support. Keep in mind that the individual might also be suffering from an undiagnosed mental health condition—at any rate, please ask them to seek additional support.

In the work that I do, I always say this prayer: "Please bring to me those that I can support in the way that I know how to support them." It is from this position that I move forward. That is not to say that I haven't experienced those who need more assistance than I can provide, but I trust that people come to see me as a part of their journey. I am able to recognize when a client may require further support.

I want to reiterate that dissociation is a natural response. It is a natural occurrence to feel as though you have stepped outside of your body and are watching yourself. It is natural to feel very numb or cold in certain situations. It is natural to forget certain things. All of this is simply the brain protecting itself. But if this is such a common thing, how do we move through it?

## GAINING MORE INSIGHT

Reflecting on the trauma cycle and understanding where it tends to be interrupted leads to insight. The trauma cycle is usually interrupted by a sense that enough time has passed that the individual should be "over" whatever happened. They may feel the need to defend their reactions and emotions, which often leads to shutting down and interrupting the trauma cycle in anticipation of being misunderstood. Remember, when an individual finally feels safe, *that* is when they will begin to react to a situation. However, modern society does not understand this concept; most people believe that when an individual is "safe," they should relax and come to terms with the situation. But it is natural for the body to come to terms with a situation via an adrenaline rush, and that energy should be expressed.

To better understand this phenomenon, consider a person who loses control of their vehicle and gets into an accident. Initially, the person will not feel the impact and/or the whiplash. When they reflect on the car accident, the person may say that everything went into slow motion. Often, it is not until the next day that their body will feel sore. That is because the individual is beginning to feel safe, as they are past the situation and at home or in a safe environment. At such a point, the consciousness returns to the body, and it is time to heal. However, the trauma cycle teaches us that when the body feels safe, it will begin to express the adrenaline rush of said accident.

This adrenaline rush is the amygdala relaxing, which allows the brain's right and left hemispheres to catch up to everything that has happened. If an individual does not complete the trauma cycle—including the adrenaline rush—a trigger is established within the subconscious. Hence, the next time the individual experiences or sees something that reminds them of the traumatic event, the amygdala gets reactivated. Only when an individual can completely express the adrenaline rush will the trauma cycle conclude. I have found that individuals feel foolish (or are looked upon as foolish) for freaking out once a situation is in the past. To prevent the trauma cycle from being interrupted, I would encourage the person to express all their feelings.

I wonder if the shadow—or a part of the shadow—is created when this natural cycle is broken or not allowed to complete itself. Maybe this aspect of the shadow helps us escape a perceived situation in order to protect us from being traumatized again.

## Approach the Shadow with Openness

When we approach shadow work and the shadow side, we will be much more successful if we approach the shadow with openness. For a moment, think about how people tend to approach a small child. The child might not necessarily be aware of their actions, nor if their behavior is deemed good or bad (acceptable or unacceptable). However, the small child will recognize if we approach them with disappointment or even anger.

As a small child, I was aware when someone was not being nice to me; I closed off or shut down. So will the shadow side. On the other hand, when I was a child, I could recognize when someone was approaching me with kindness and wanted to be my friend. I was drawn to this approach. Yes, I am comparing the shadow side to a child, but not because I believe it to be young or immature. Rather, I am comparing it to a child from the perspective that the shadow hasn't been paid attention to and is not necessarily socialized due to the fact that it has been hidden away.

If we approach the shadow with openness, compassion, and a willingness to learn from it—the same way one might approach a small child—the shadow will respond to this approach in a positive way. Remember, the shadow side is the aspect of ourselves that has been neglected, ignored, rejected, and hidden away. Naturally, the shadow will be leery of our intentions at first. This is why I wrote this book—so that we may meet our shadow side and learn from it.

### My Experience with My Shadow

As I shared previously, approaching the shadow with kindness is key. To illustrate this, here is a story about a time I met one aspect of my shadow side.

When I was around thirty-five years old, I had a dream. I dreamt of four-year-old me. She was adorable, with pigtails and all. In my dream, she had opened the refrigerator and was reaching up to get some snacks to eat. At this point in the dream, I was not seeing things from her perspective; instead, I was in the position of her parent.

Much to my surprise, my first reaction was to yell at four-year-old me. "What do you think you are doing, young lady? Those snacks are not for you! They are for our community!" (*Hmm*...I was raised by the pastor of a church, so there were always snacks for our community that I wasn't allowed to eat.)

In the dream, my four-year-old self did not like what I said, nor my approach. She yelled back at me, "When is it going to be MY TURN?!"

I was in disbelief. I would have never raised my voice to any adult at that stage in my life—I was a "good little preacher's kid." I opened my mouth to yell at her and tell her that I was going to wash her mouth out with soap and give her a spanking. But just before this automatic response came out of my mouth, I stopped.

I looked at my four-year-old self and knelt down in front of her. I said, "You are right—it is your turn now!"

I abruptly woke up from my dream and reflected on it. I realized that there was an aspect of myself that was angry that it was never my turn, that I was raised to give all my things away and to be proud of the fact that I considered myself last. When I was growing up, I was told that my given name, Joy, was an acronym for Jesus first, Others second, and Yourself last. Hence, it was drilled into me that it was never going to be my turn. With great sadness and also a great understanding of four-year-old me, I decided that I was going to stop believing that I was not allowed to take part in the "snacks" of life, and that I got a turn too.

My shadow was not my four-year-old self, nor was my shadow the parental figure. My shadow was the aspect of myself that was angry yet had to hide this fact. Sometimes, the shadow is simply seeking justice for the rest of the self that didn't know it was allowed justice. At least in this instance it was.

This dream changed me and my life moving forward. I still rejoice when it is other people's turn, but now I take my turn too. I am more balanced because of this experience.

### Anger Is Natural

Being raised by a reverend made me resistant to certain words and feelings, one being the feeling of anger. I was taught to pray for those who wronged me; I was taught to turn the other cheek. I understand that these are valuable lessons in certain situations, but as I mature, I recognize that anger is natural, and it should not be ignored or denied. It is part of life.

From a shamanic approach, I work with the natural world. The natural world is my teacher and helps me understand life's wisdom. For example, when a momma bear is protecting her cubs, she doesn't sit back as if to say, "I will pray for the predator that is trying to eat my children." Nope! Without being taught, she will defend her cubs. This is one of many ways that the natural world shows us that anger is natural when it is necessary.

I think anger needs to be kept in check when we have denied ourselves of anger in certain situations, which leads to it building up inside us. This type of buildup will inevitably come out too strongly, likely during the wrong situation and at the wrong time. But how are we to navigate embracing our anger if we were taught not to feel it? When I feel angry, I understand that it is anger that I am feeling. I don't place it on myself or another person, but I do place it on the situation. For example, "I hate it when such-and-such happens" versus "I hate that person because of what they did to me." This approach takes shame and blame out of the situation while still allowing anger to cycle through naturally.

## HISTORICAL AND ANCESTRAL TRAUMAS

There are many different types of traumas. Trauma is not a quantitative experience; it is not something that can be numerically measured. Trauma is a qualitative experience—something that is measured within the mind, emotions, and within the body and the soul. Some types of traumas are a one-time experience. Other types of traumatic experiences happen over a period of time. In any case, trauma is a signal that life is no longer going to be the same. This includes historical trauma(s), which is also known as ancestral trauma(s)—trauma from the past that is passed down generationally.

Historical trauma is a cultural, racial, and ethnic type of trauma that is multigenerational and passed down from generation to generation. I have experienced historical trauma due to the fact that I am Native American and Indigenous. In my youth, I felt safer behaving like others within my given community, which was a white-bodied community. I was afraid to be myself; I was afraid to "look" Native. This was not a natural fear; it developed when I recognized that I was different and felt ashamed that I was Navajo. At this time in my life, it is cool to be Navajo—but I grew up at a time when it wasn't accepted.

You do not need to be Navajo or Indigenous to understand this concept. At this point in history, you can simply be different—the kind of "different" that pushes and challenges the status quo. This type of trauma is less tangible but just as real! Maybe what I am speaking about goes beyond cultural, racial, and ethnic understandings; maybe it seeps into self-expression and sexual orientation too. We still have a ways to go in order to understand the trauma that nonacceptance and annihilation of groups will cause to the body and the soul.

Historical trauma and ancestral trauma can be hard to identify, yet they are as valid as any other type of trauma. Just because a traumatic experience didn't happen directly to an individual does not mean that this traumatic experience isn't held within their DNA. The individual may not understand why they are reacting a certain way, yet their reaction is true. If we can hold this understanding within our consciousness, we may be able to create a safer and healthier world for others.

When I visualize what historical or ancestral trauma look like, I see a tree. A tree that has grown over centuries. A tree that is rooted in the soil of old ways of thinking, old ways of understanding. These old ways of thinking and understanding need to be challenged—tilled—if the tree is to remain healthy and aerated. Otherwise, root rot will occur.

# 3

# THE SHAMAN

One does not need to be a shaman in order to read this book, let alone to perform shadow work. However, this book provides a guide for shadow work from my shamanic perspective. Again, this is *my* perspective—shamanism and shamanic practitioners come in all shapes and sizes. In this chapter, we will cover the etymology of the term *shaman*, explain a variety of shamanic concepts, and take a look at what shamans do. Most importantly, we are going to look at the ethics that a balanced shaman will abide by.

## ORIGIN OF THE TERM *SHAMAN*

I define *shamanism* as a global term used to describe an individual whose daily and spiritual practices are rooted in working with the natural world and the elements to bring healing and balance to self and others. But where did the word *shaman* come from? The term *shaman* dates back to the late–seventeenth century German word *Schaman* and, a few decades later, the Russian word *šaman*. The German word *Schaman* meant "a sorcerer or priest."[4]

You may be surprised to learn that the term *shaman* is global and did not originate from the Indigenous people of North America. It is not that Indigenous peoples didn't have a shaman—rather, we did not use that word. Post colonialism, the term *shaman* simply describes an individual who works with the natural world to bring balance and healing to self and others.

There are all kinds of shamans: Peruvian Shamans, European Shamans, African Shamans, etc. Moreover, there are traditional shamans within any given culture; they are the practitioners who practice their culturally recognized ceremonial ways. There is also neoshamanism, which is more of a personally developed shamanic practice versus a cultural expression. I am not here to tell you who is "allowed" to be a shaman and who is not, as that is not my place. I believe that is the job of the spirits within the natural world.

At this point, I would like to let you know that there is a school of thought that a "true" shaman does not call themselves a shaman, but a shamanic practitioner. I am not here to tell you to adopt this school of thought or to reject it—I am here to bring awareness. Some believe that an individual can refer to themselves as a shaman. Personally, I have been asked "Are you a shaman?" I responded, "Until they stop calling me that, I suppose I am." If someone recognizes me as such, I will agree. In short, how

---

4. *Oxford English Dictionary Online*, "shaman," accessed July 30, 2024, https://www.oed.com/dictionary/shaman_n.

we move in the world is reflected in the titles that people call us. People started to call me a shaman, and so I am until I am not. When I am not a shaman anymore, it will be because I no longer am recognized as such—I will no longer be earning the title.

I am of the Navajo Nation and come from a long line of medicine people. This is not to suggest that all Navajo medicine people will work with the shadow, but I do. What I practice can be seen as taboo; traditional Navajo teachings discourage thinking or talking about darker topics, including skinwalkers,[5] taboo animals like snakes, and the shadow. A traditional Navajo individual will literally walk out of the room if one of these topics is brought up! What I was told by my father is that "such topics" will toss you out of balance, and it will toss those who hear about those topics out of balance as well. Additionally, when one speaks about taboo topics, they call that taboo spirit to them, and bad things can happen because of their thoughts and speech. I cannot disagree with this; however, I am not a traditional Navajo medicine person. I have been referred to by the elders outside of the Navajo Nation as "the silhouette of the future medicine person." I have a unique perspective.

## SHAMANIC CONCEPTS

In this section, I will cover some of the general, global concepts that a shaman or shamanic practitioner would be familiar with.

---

5. *Skinwalker* is a Navajo term meaning "a malevolent person with supernatural powers who assumes the appearance of a wolf, coyote, or other animal by wearing its skin" (*Oxford English Dictionary Online*, "skinwalker," accessed March 1, 2024, https://www.oed.com/dictionary/skinwalker_n).

## Animism

Animism is the belief that every natural thing has a soul and is alive in one way or another. This would include you and me, all animals, all plants, all crystals, all landscapes, all seasons, all weather patterns, etc. The tools that you carry are alive. The elements that you work with are alive. The cosmos that pulls you is alive. Everything has a life force and holds a consciousness at one level or another.

I have found that things that were constructed from natural components, such as a wooden table or chair, hold characteristics and spirits of their own; this could even apply to a room in your home. Hence, when you approach any natural organism, treat it with respect. Of course, this includes the shadow. I invite you to look at the world through this lens and see how everything shifts.

## All Is Energy

As shared previously, all is energy. This is not a philosophy—this is actual science. Everything, at its base, is energy. The natural world holds this understanding and continues to balance and rebalance the energy within it. We can learn from this concept. One nature-based understanding is that energy is positive and negative. These terms are not synonymous with "good" and "bad." For example, positive ionic charge in an environment will weaken the body's natural strength, creating depression, anxiety, and fatigue. Positive ions increase with higher pollution, toxic chemicals, and mold. On the other hand, negative ionic charge within an environment will increase levels of serotonin in the body, alleviating depression, anxiety, and fatigue. Negative ions increase by the ocean, within a forest, and even by a waterfall. Hence, we must release the idea that energy that is positive is "good" and energy that is negative is "bad." Energy is neither "good" nor "bad"—it just is. This understanding can rebalance our approach to energy.

And so it is with the shadow. It is energy. It should not be understood as bad. It is dark like the night; it is obscure like the outer planets; it is natural like the shade of a tree. What if we were to release the labels we assign to the shadow and, instead, let it show us what it is?

## Energy Is Sacred

Building off the previous shamanic concept, I would like to share that energy is sacred. Whether I am comfortable with a certain energy or uncomfortable with the energy isn't the point—the point is that energy is sacred and should be treated as such. This is a very important concept to understand when you are doing shadow work. The shadow is energy, and as such, it is sacred. Through journey work, you will begin to recognize, acknowledge, understand, and respect it for what it is.

## Balance

As mentioned previously, the concept of balance is key for a shaman. To learn about balance, we look to our greatest teacher: the natural world. The day balances with the night over the course of a year. On the winter solstice, we experience the longest night of the year, and the summer solstice is the longest day. Likewise, we find balancing and rebalancing within the ecosystem. For example, in the winter season, many ecosystems grow cold and plants go dormant. Animals may change their hunting or sleeping schedules to accommodate the colder environment. However, in the summer season, plants will develop and grow, and animals may give birth to new life. Additionally, there is balance to be found in the yin-yang, which flows within everything. The yin represents chaos energy, night energy, moon energy, and feminine energy, and its opposite is the yang, which represents the energy of order, the energy of the day, the energy of the sun, and masculine energy. As we work with the shadow, we must greet it as part of our natural balance: the night-self to our day-self.

It is important to remember that blocked energy cannot balance or rebalance itself, which causes disease and discord. As shamanic practitioners, we need to learn how to unblock energy so that it can balance itself; energy will naturally rebalance if it is not hindered or blocked.

## Many Worlds

Shamans recognize that there is more than one world. In fact, there are many worlds—worlds that go beyond physical space and time, magical worlds where we can sit with ourselves, others, and deities. Many shamans work within three main worlds: the upper world, the middle world, and the lower world. In my personal experience, the upper world is where one can connect with guides, deities, and the Divine, accessing wisdom and knowledge. The middle world is the three-dimensional reality we all recognize here on Earth. The lower world is where one can take action to affect reality and rebalance energy. It is also the place we can connect with our roots and basic instincts. In each of these worlds, an individual is able to affect change in the other worlds.

Like the butterfly effect, changing things in one space and time will effect change in the larger system. My first book, *The Journey of the Soul: The Path of a Medicine Person*, goes into more detail about the three worlds.

However, we should not limit ourselves to merely three worlds. I have found that there are countless worlds that a shaman can access and enter. Although the concept of the worlds may vary within different shamanic paths, the idea of being able to "journey" into other worlds (other realms) in order to restore balance is very common.

Before journeying into any world, I recommend setting the ego aside and journeying with intent. When I speak of ego here, I am not speaking about setting your true self aside; I am speaking about setting your projected self aside. Do your homework on the customs of the world that you would like to journey to—understand the ways of that world. It is respectful and honorable to do so, just like researching a different country to understand the culture before traveling there. Although it is possible for an individual to spontaneously decide to journey to a world at any time, it is ill-advised to do so because they will inevitably encounter something they aren't prepared for. My advice is to travel with intent and with respect for the world that you are about to enter.

There are as many worlds as there are cultural understandings, ceremonial practices, and healing modalities. For example, there are nine worlds in Norse culture. Hence, a ceremonial practitioner of this esoteric wisdom would understand and be able to move through each of the nine worlds in order to affect change and restore balance. In Kabbalah, there are ten different worlds under the Tree of Life, or ten different spheres (sephirot). A mystic on this path would be able to recognize and navigate these ten realms. I would also like to mention the basic seven-chakra system. Although the chakra system has recently grown in popularity due to yoga practices and other health-conscious endeavors, its origins are in ancient India, dating back thousands of years. As a shaman who works with the seven-chakra system, I might find myself wanting to move within my own individual chakras as a shamanic realm or world. Or, with permission, I might be invited into another's chakra system for the purpose of understanding or healing. I know that the chakras are not usually seen as separate realms or worlds, but from my experience as a shaman, the chakra system does indeed have many worlds. Finally, I would like to mention the four bodies of existence or realms of knowledge: physical, emotional, mental, and spiritual. I learned this concept from the medicine people of the Navajo Nation. Hence, I categorize it as a shamanic worldview.

The concept of many worlds applies to the shadow as well. As a shaman, I believe that the shadow is alive and lives in a separate state of consciousness. Hence, we will need to journey to the state of consciousness (or world) that the shadow exists in.

I offer this information to illustrate that there are many different worlds and worldviews to consider as we begin to understand the word *shamanism* as an overarching terminology. In doing so, we must consider both traditional shamanism and neoshamanism. I practice both. As a traditional shaman, I draw from my bloodline and understand the four bodies of existence. I also have become a neoshaman, as I have drawn correlations beyond what my culture taught me, such as working with the chakra system.

## WHAT DO SHAMANS DO?

Shamanism tends to be more of a solo practice than a group practice. Whereas groups, churches, covens, and kindreds do rituals and ceremonies together, a shaman will embark on a journey solo, then guide others on their personal or group journey. I highly recommend taking a personal journey to discover your shadow before even considering taking anyone else on this journey. Not only is this a responsible practice, but it will also provide you with more insight into the experience of shadow work. In working with your own shadow, you become more adept, more acquainted, and more effective. We learn so much by exploring the lay of the land ourselves—there is so much more wisdom within the experiencing of it than simply reading about it.

There are many answers to the question of what a shaman does. However, I would say that universally, one of the most common things a shaman does is work as an intermediary between the worlds; they communicate between worlds in order to affect change on the earthly plane. Ultimately, a shaman acts as an intermediary to bring balance.

Most shamanic practitioners work with the natural world and the spirits of the natural world to affect the human world. Shamans tend to perceive things in a different way than the average human being will see and understand. In this book, I have focused on working with the four worlds of the human experience (physical, emotional, mental, spiritual) and the seven basic chakras.

## THE FOUR BODIES/WORLDS OF THE HUMAN EXPERIENCE

There are physical, emotional, mental, and spiritual aspects of the self and the human experience. As a shaman, I refer to these as the four bodies of existence. I refer to them as "bodies" because it assists us in understanding that each of these needs to be cared for like a body: with food, exercise, and rest. Here are some examples of what caring for each of the four bodies looks like.

The physical body needs food, exercise, and rest. Healthy food for the physical body is necessary to provide us with the nutrition that we need to be healthy and strong. The physical body needs a certain amount of exercise in order to stay limber and fit. We also need an adequate night's rest in order to fully function the next day. As we sleep, the physical body (including the brain) will be able to heal, repair, and clear out any waste.

The emotional body also needs food, exercise, and rest, but in a different way. The emotional body needs to be nourished. We need to feel safe, accepted for who we are, and loved. We need to exercise this body by understanding and relating to others, extending beyond our own emotional needs. We also need to rest the emotional body in a safe place where we can relax and laugh and play. When we rest the emotional body, deeper understanding will be the reward: a proactive emotional body versus a reactive emotional body. We will be able to self-regulate our emotions rather than responding to the world from a position of emotional exhaustion.

The mental body needs food, exercise, and rest. It is "fed" through learning and engaging with new ideas and concepts; it needs to be inspired. The mental body exercises by considering new ideas, often entertained yet not adopted. This allows for the expansion of the mental capacity. And, of course, the mental body needs to rest. We must make time to relax and release our thoughts via meditation or by performing a task that relaxes the mind. Giving the mind time to rest is something that is natural and, at times, is needed for our mental health. Additionally, when I take a mental break from something, it allows for creation as new thought processes or ideas come through. Resting the mental body is essential.

Finally, the spiritual body also needs food, exercise, and rest. Food for the spiritual body is gained through silent prayer and consideration of something larger than ourselves—a seeking of higher understanding in order to evolve or become enlightened. Spiritual enlightenment does not only come from religion; at times, it comes through science, a natural phenomenon of synchronized events, or recognition of a larger pattern. Basically, spiritual enlightenment is a larger understanding revealing itself so that we continue to believe in something more than ourselves. This practice is both food and exercise for the spiritual body, as it needs to practice believing. The art of believing is the exercise. The spiritual body also needs rest. Rest is a time to relax and engage in a simple, mundane task in order to allow spirit to reach out to you (a symbiotic relationship). When I engage in spiritual rest, I practice silence within. It is at these times that spirit will come to me and say, "You have sought me out. Now, rest, and I will seek you too. We are connected. We are one. This is love."

A shamanic understanding of the four bodies of existence is revealed within the *Vitruvian Man*, an image by Leonardo da Vinci. This figure provides us with a visual of the perfect proportions of the human body, including mathematical and geometrical equations. However, from a shamanic point of view, when I look at this image, I see a perfect representation of the four bodies of existence. This image shows us that all four bodies of existence are within us, but each holds their individual space.

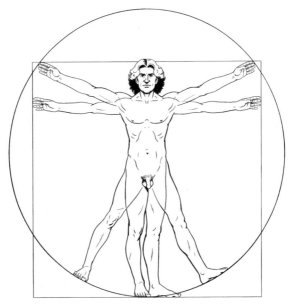

The *Vitruvian Man*

The physical body is depicted by a man whose arms are extended outward, with the legs together directly beneath him. The emotional body is depicted by the arms that are raised up and the feet that are outstretched; this represents movement or motion. I remember that this is the emotional body by thinking that *motion* sounds like *emotion*. The mental body is depicted by the square that surrounds the man's body. Finally, the spiritual body is depicted by the large circle that surrounds everything else—i.e., it contains the other bodies.

## Out of Balance

If one of the four bodies is out of balance, it will toss all the other bodies out of balance as well. Hence, as a shaman, I run diagnostics. With the permission of the client, I tap into each of their four bodies to understand them. First, I perceive their physical body to see if there is any blockage. Then, I do the same with their emotional, mental, and spiritual bodies. At times, I perceive an imbalance or blockage in one of their bodies. (I could write a whole book about how to spot an imbalance, and it wouldn't even scratch the surface!) Practitioners from different specialties spot an imbalance within someone's system in different ways: a doctor can spot an imbalance through their skillset, a psychologist will detect an imbalance using their skillset, and friends and family can detect an imbalance simply because they are familiar with an individual's balanced aspects. I can even spot an imbalance within myself! Basically, I recognize an imbalance when the four bodies aren't naturally and organically moving as one. One or more of the four bodies is stuck or shut down, and the system needs to be rebalanced. This imbalance might reveal itself as insomnia, anxiety, depression, etc.

If I detect an imbalance, I gently assist the imbalanced body to do what it naturally wants to do. Remember, all is energy, and energy seeks its freedom. Hence, I help the energy within the affected body become safe and free in order to express itself. Inevitably, the other bodies will follow suit, and natural balance will be restored with the alignment of all four bodies. At times, this is what a shaman does when they journey into other worlds. As a neoshaman, I also work with the seven chakras to restore balance.

# THE CHAKRA SYSTEM

Chakras are known as vital energy points of life force. It is believed that at the inner core of each one of us spin seven main energy centers called chakras. In Sanskrit, the meaning of the word *chakra* is "wheel" or "disk."[6] Each of these chakras reflects an aspect of essential consciousness. Moreover, chakras have three main functions: to receive energy, to assimilate energy, and to transmit or express energy.[7] In this section, I have provided an overview of each of the seven chakras. If you would like a more detailed look at the chakra system, there are many credible books and teachers who delve deeper into this topic. However, this quick overview of the chakra system will provide you with what you need to know in order to become a shadow worker and work with the tools within this book.

| Chakra | Keyword(s) | Color | The Right to Be or Assertion |
|---|---|---|---|
| Root | Survival | Red | "I have the right to be here" |
| Sacral | Sexuality | Orange | "I have the right to connect" |
| Solar plexus | Free will | Yellow | "I have the right to be me" |
| Heart | Love and unity | Green | "I have the right to love and to be loved" |

6. Judith, *Wheels of Life*, 16.

7. Judith, *Wheels of Life*, 24.

| Chakra | Keyword(s) | Color | The Right to Be or Assertion |
|--------|-----------|-------|------------------------------|
| Throat | Communication | Blue | "I have the right to express" |
| Third eye | Intuition | Indigo | "I have the right to perceive" |
| Crown | Consciousness | Purple, white | "I am one with everything" |

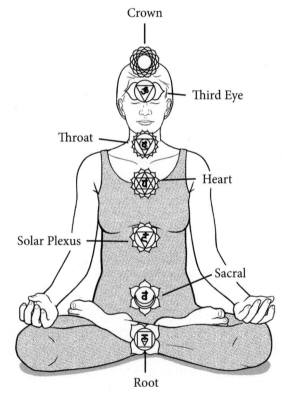

The chakras

The chakra system is a very ancient understanding of the inner workings of the human experience. Chakras provide a road map that can show us what we need to survive, how we need to connect, how to express and receive love, how to better express ourselves, etc. They are foundational points of personal self-expression. In addition to assisting us with personal development, the chakra system also assists with our connections to others and to the Divine.

Working with the seven chakras can provide a clearer picture of the interplay of the four bodies of existence. The seven chakras give us a deeper, fuller, and more profound formula for wholeness that integrates the physical, emotional, mental, and spiritual bodies. The seven chakras and the four bodies of existence flow in tandem. For example, the root chakra of survival can and will appear in each of the four bodies. In the physical body, the root chakra asks, "How can I physically survive?" In the emotional body, the root chakra asks, "How can I emotionally survive?" In the mental body, the root chakra asks, "How can I mentally survive?" In the spiritual body, the root chakra asks, "How can I spiritually survive?" Each of the seven chakras appears in each of the four bodies; this offers a very basic—yet dynamic—understanding of how complex the human experience can be.

In this book, we will be working with the four bodies of existence to understand ourselves and others physically, emotionally, mentally, and spiritually. At times, we will reflect on the seven-chakra system to gain a fuller understanding of other aspects that could be affected during shadow work. You will learn to perfect your ability to work with these realms and worlds as an intermediary, and to journey within these realms.

## JOURNEY WORK

Journey work is a significant part of the shamanic experience, and the way we breathe is a crucial part of supporting journey work. In this section, I will explore the importance of breathwork and recommend a specific exercise. While reading this section of the book, keep in mind that later on, you will be asked to "breathe in this place" a number of times. This phrase simply means to pause and focus on your breath as you take in your surroundings.

### The Threefold Breath

The threefold breath is an exercise that simultaneously benefits the physical, emotional, mental, and spiritual bodies. First, inhale through the nose. Second, hold the breath within the physical body. Third, exhale through the mouth. (Inhaling through the nose and exhaling through the mouth will activate the parasympathetic nervous system, which aids in relaxation and counteracts the amygdala's flight, fright, or freeze responses.) Each of these three steps lasts for a certain number of counts that work best for the individual. For example, the cadence of a threefold breath may be: inhale for four counts, hold for four counts, and exhale for six counts. I encourage every individual to find the count and cadence that works best for them.

In addition to practicing the threefold breath before and during journey work, I also recommend practicing it whenever you enter the natural world in order to relax and connect with your surroundings. It is a wonderful practice to do throughout your day in order to focus and center yourself.

## States of Consciousness

Breathwork is really important because it can actually alter our brain waves. Normally, a human's brain waves are detected by an electroencephalogram (EEG) between thirteen and twenty hertz, depending on the individual's mental state in that moment. When we begin to relax, the oscillation slows down. However, even though we are "slowing down," so to speak, slower brain waves actually cause us to become more aware of our surroundings as we ground and center. This is the perfect zone for guided meditation and journey work. The oscillation continues to slow down as we begin to drift off to sleep and, eventually, we fall asleep. Here is a basic list of states of consciousness that each of us enters.

- **Beta state** is when an individual is fully awake and completely active. In this state, brain waves detected by an EEG are between thirteen and twenty hertz. This state of consciousness is what we experience on any given day.

- **Alpha state** is when an individual's mind is relaxed and the person has entered a more focused, expanded state of awareness. Although it might sound contradictory that a slower alpha brain wave is more focused than the faster beta brain wave, it is accurate. Think of how your brain functions when you are rushing around multitasking versus when you are able to slow down and focus. This is the difference between beta state and alpha state. In alpha state, the brain waves detected by an EEG are between eight and thirteen hertz. This speed is more of a meditative state of consciousness.

- **Theta state** is when an individual relaxes even more, to the point of drowsiness. The mind has entered a region that correlates with brain wave patterns of between four and eight hertz. While in theta state, one can experience profound creativity characterized by feelings of inspiration and spirituality.

- **Delta state** is the level at which the differentiated self (ego) expands to become undifferentiated and operates outside of the confines of linear time/space. This is also recognized as deep sleep. In delta state, brain waves oscillate up to four hertz.[8]

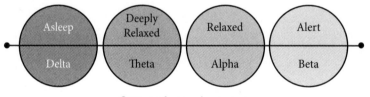

States of consciousness

Working with the threefold breath can take us from beta state into alpha state. An alpha state is a more relaxed state that still impacts all four bodies. Some of the many benefits of alpha state include deep relaxation of the emotional and mental bodies, increased levels of creativity, more focus and improved problem-solving skills, increased ability to learn something new,

8. Xavier, Ting, and Fauzan, "Exploratory Study of Brain Waves."

and increased serotonin levels. Serotonin is a neurotransmitter produced in the brain that directly impacts mood, contributing to a sense of well-being and happiness.

## Performing Journey Work

As a shaman journeys into various spaces and times—into various states of consciousness—a shaman has the ability to ground and center in each place. But a shaman needs to find some familiarity within each place in order to move forward. Awareness is key. The first step is to "breathe in this place." Take it all in, for we have journeyed into a different world, a world of wonder.

Here is one way to naturally journey: Do the breathwork exercises mentioned previously. Inhale, hold, exhale. Continue to do this breathwork for one to three minutes or until you feel completely relaxed. This will take you into the alpha state of consciousness. Here is where you can connect more deeply with your imagination. Imagination is the portal through which we can access other worlds. It is the point of entry.

Sometimes adults doubt the power of imagination. If we set the intent to allow the Divine to work with our imagination, it moves from a make-believe place to a sacred place. Within this sacred place, spirit drives our thoughts and opens the door to other worlds that are very real and tangible. What was once imagination becomes the gateway to that which lies beyond. There is a place beyond good and evil, beyond the mundane world, beyond three-dimensional reality—the shaman will meet you there.

It takes practice and experience to understand how powerful journey work is. Historically, the initiation of a shaman involved being left alone for a night within the depths of the woods. At first, the initiate's imagination would run wild as all their wildest hopes and darkest fears rose from within. In the past, this would have been a literal practice; now, we use the same concept, but it is experienced metaphorically. We reflect on the times in life when we felt as though we were all alone in the dark. Part of the initiation into shamanic journeying is facing our darkest fears, and fear will run rampant until the shaman learns how to surrender. Shamanic practitioners learn how to let go and relax into the journey itself.

The key to journeying is to slow down the thinking process. Ground within the journey by placing one foot in front of the other. Take in the entire lay of the land. Each of us knows how to naturally jump in and out of places within our own memory, within our thoughts, within our imagination. In the same way, the skill of the shaman is to slow down and allow the world's landscape to unfold before them. Again, this is not about speed; it is all about slowing down and surrendering to the journey.

When you begin to experience something that you were not expecting to experience, that is when you will begin to recognize that there is something else—*someone* else, another energy—that is at play within the journey. Additionally, the more that you journey, the more you will notice the effects that your journey work has manifested into three-dimensional reality. As long as you set an intention and turn over your journey to the Divine, you will be in good hands. This is how spirit can reveal things to you beyond your ordinary world and understanding.

### *My Personal Journey Experience*

Here is an example of my development within journey work. When the spirit of the shaman called to me to learn more, I was in my adulthood. I was inspired to journey to the underworld, but in order for me to do so, I needed to find my "power spot."

Power spots are like the earth's ley lines. Ley lines are invisible (or as some would say, imaginary) lines within the earth that hold more power or more energy. A power spot is the same concept, yet it is a point in the natural world that draws an individual.

Power spots can be found in many different locations; they are not limited to one place or landscape. If you have ever visited a new location and been drawn to an area that felt comfortable to you, you may have found a power spot. For example, when taking a walk in the natural world, you might be drawn to a certain place to sit and relax, whether it is under a tree, by a river, or on a rock.

With that being said, a true power spot is found intentionally. An individual looks for this special place in the natural world with the intention of meditating in that spot or recalling that spot in future meditations.

If you find your power spot in a place where you feel comfortable meditating, please do so. However, at times you might find a power spot that you aren't able to take the time to meditate at, or the power spot may be too public, with people walking past and other distractions. Maybe you do not feel comfortable meditating in your power spot due to external exposures. This is not a problem! Stand in that power spot you've found and connect with the energy. Feel the vibration of it, and memorize it. Then, from the comfort of your own home, you can recall your power spot and visualize returning to it in order to feel its direct power.

I found my power spot in my own backyard. I looked around my yard and was drawn to a specific large stone. I can't explain how except to say that I was drawn to it. However, there was traffic going by, and I could not completely relax and go into meditation. So, once I had found my power spot, I went indoors to begin my journey.

I don't really know if this was the first time I ever did journey work, but it certainly was the first time I called it that! I began to listen to the sound of prerecorded drumming, laid down on the couch, and relaxed. With the assistance of the drumbeat, I was able to slow down and focus. I imagined myself getting up from the couch, walking down the steps of my home, and slowly walking into my backyard. I visualized sitting in the power spot that I had identified earlier. I rested into my power spot and began to move down into the earth.

As I moved through the earth, I could feel the soil and roots from plants. I was present within every moment. Suddenly, I dropped into a different place and a different time. I found myself on the side of a cliff. The cliff was made from the red rocks of the desert. I looked out across the horizon and spotted a hogan (traditional dwelling of the Navajo people). I could see a middle-aged Navajo man standing outside of the hogan. I wanted to go to him. The desire to see him moved me into the air, and I flew toward him. It was awesome—I could fly! I landed on a perch beside him, and he knew that I was there. I realized then that I was in the form of a raven. I connected with this space and time—this journey, or what some would call a meditation.

As is typical of journeying and meditation work, I often came out of it like a dream. Once I took in enough information, I would return to my physical body and reflect on the experience.

For months, I naturally went on this journey, learning every-thing I could from this man via my meditative practice every morning. It was one of the most wonderful experiences. How-ever, I still was under the impression that it was all in my imag-ination, but it was so pleasant that it didn't matter to me where these experiences came from. The man was my teacher; he was my shaman. He taught me so much. I learned about energy, rit-uals, and tools. Throughout my meditative practice, he worked with me and showed me things—we rarely spoke in words. We more so spoke through understanding each other's actions.

One day, I decided to perform journey work to see my grand-mother and Aunt Alice on the Navajo reservation. Both were medicine women. At this point in time, my grandmother had passed on, although I had known her in my lifetime, while Aunt Alice was still alive in this physical realm. (As I am writing this book, my aunt Alice now lives in the realm of my grandmother.) Seeing them again was simply an idea that popped into my head. I thought, *Why not imagine spending time with them?* With this intention, I did the same thing that I had been doing to meet my shaman: I listened to the drums, visualized walking to my power spot, and dropped down to the Navajo reservation. This time I saw a hogan and entered it. Inside were my grandmother and Aunt Alice. We sat in a circle together and held hands and had a wonderful time. Toward the end of this visit, Aunt Alice handed me a stone. I thought, *How sweet*, and I came out of my medita-tive state after less than thirty minutes.

The next week, I received a package in the mail from the Navajo reservation. It was addressed to me by my aunt Alice. I opened it up, and there was a stone! Attached was a short note that said, "Could it be that the creator created us to be a perfect circle?" I was so stunned! I could barely believe what had just happened. In that moment, I knew that my imagination—or shall I say my journey work—was real. Wow! From that point on, I understood the power of journey work.

Additionally, I later realized that the shaman who I was going to see was none other than my grandfather, a medicine man. My grandfather was known to carry the spirit of Corvidae (i.e., crows, ravens, etc.). Hence, I am called Granddaughter Crow.

## Alternate States

Shamans may enter alternate states to begin journey work. There are several ways to achieve an alternate state, which is a state that allows us to view reality from a different perspective. Earlier, we examined a very natural way to move into another state of consciousness via breathwork: moving from beta to alpha state of consciousness can help us relax and focus. This is just one way that a shaman can open the passageway to other worlds.

There are other methods that some shamans work with to access other worlds: plant-assisted journeying. I am not recommending any of the following methods, nor am I discouraging any of them. If you are interested in partaking in any one of these methods, I strongly advise that you do your homework and find a credible shaman or doctor who can watch over you as you journey.

### Peyote

Earlier, I introduced my aunt Alice. When Aunt Alice walked this earth, she did so as a high priestess of the Peyote Way. Peyote is a small cactus that grows in the desert areas of North America. When ingested, it causes hallucinations. However, when prepared by a medicine person (usually as a tea), peyote is believed to create a spiritually guided hallucination that allows an individual to achieve a deeper understanding of themselves and their soul's journey. To partake of the peyote is sacred, and Aunt Alice was the shaman that would watch over people within this cultural ceremony. This is something that is cultural to the Navajo people, as well as other cultures. As a sacred psychedelic, peyote needs to be respected and approached with the right intention. As insightful as a peyote ceremony might be, it can also be a terrifying experience if the individual isn't ready for the ceremony.

### Ayahuasca

Like the peyote, ayahuasca is a psychedelic that is to be treated with great respect. Ayahuasca is made by combining different plant substances in a ritualistic manner in order to connect an individual to the natural world and to themselves. Just like with peyote, ayahuasca can be enlightening or frightening. Hence, it needs to be respected. Administered by a shaman in a sacred ayahuasca ceremony, this energy can be a powerful way to reach other states of consciousness. In recent years, ayahuasca has been studied to determine its usefulness as a pharmacological and therapeutic substance.[9]

### Magic Mushrooms

Another earth-based plant is the magic mushroom, or psilocybin mushrooms. Magic mushrooms grow all around the world, excluding Antarctica. Because they are global, medicine people

9. Ruffell et al., "Ayahuasca."

around the world have worked with magic mushrooms for generations. Due to the widespread nature of these mushrooms, it is good to note that there are many kinds of psilocybin mushrooms.

Psilocybin has been studied for its ability to assist with ailments such as depression.[10] However, psilocybin mushrooms are illegal in many parts of the world. Please do your research to understand whether it is legal or illegal to work with psilocybin mushrooms in your community.

### *Pure Intention and Sacred Respect*

However you decide to move into an alternate state, do so with pure intention and sacred respect. If you choose to work with threefold breathwork, blessings to you on your journey. If you choose to work with Peyote, please do so under the guidance of a traditional shaman. If you choose to work with Ayahuasca, do so under the care of a traditional shaman or a certified medical practitioner. If you choose to partake in magic mushrooms, please honor the medicine and where it has come from: the earth. Do what you will, with harm to none. Happy journey.

## SPIRITUAL ETHICS

Another important aspect of the shamanic experience is upholding spiritual ethics. Spiritual ethics are much like ethics within the physical realm. For example, imagine that you are walking down the street and see that there is a person sitting on a bench waiting for the bus. This individual is wearing a hat and sunglasses and

---

10. Goldberg et al., "The Experimental Effects of Psilocybin on Symptoms of Anxiety and Depression."

appears to be relaxed. You would not be inclined to walk over to that person and say, "I see that you have a hat and sunglasses on. Does that mean that you are trying to keep the sun out of your eyes? Would you like an umbrella to keep the sun off you?" That exchange would be socially awkward, as it is unnecessary; the person was simply minding their own business.

So it is within the spiritual realm. If I am walking down the street and encounter a stranger, I may pick up on certain energy that makes me feel like I could assist them in healing themselves. However, imagine how I would make someone feel if I, a total stranger, approached them because I peered into their energetic field without their permission. It is not ethical to do so. This would create a very uncomfortable feeling for the individual and is an invasion of their personal space and life.

This actually has happened to me. Strangers have come up to me and started psychically reading me without my permission. At times, they simply started trying to manipulate my personal space and energy without my permission. This is an intrusive way to behave as a spiritual practitioner, be it shamanism or any other spiritual gift. I understand that when our gifts open up, it is so wonderful to be able to see the energy of another. However, we should always ask for permission to engage with them and their energetic field. We can't let excitement overtake the situation and cross boundaries. Always ask if someone would like to have a reading or a healing. This shows them respect, and now the ball is in their court.

Here is another example of spiritual ethics. Imagine walking down the street and overhearing two people who are talking. You have thoughts on what they are talking about and may want to interject your opinion. Would it be nice to walk up to them and simply interject yourself and your opinion into their conversation? No, it would be rude. A lot of the time, spiritual workers have a sense that if they pick up on something, it is their responsibility to interject. This is not so. You see because you are a seer; you hear because your clairaudient. You may walk through the physical realm and perceive something, but please only go where you are invited. Otherwise, you will shut others down and turn them off to the gifts of the healers.

Individuals who always give their unsolicited opinions shut other people down. It is the same energetic exchange in the spiritual realm. With this being said, please feel free to pray for people's health and well-being, etc. However, recognize that spirit is moving in their life in ways that we may not necessarily understand. Send love and light, but be careful not to manipulate energy if you have not been asked to.

So, what is one to do if they pick up on something? Do nothing unless they are asked? Well, when I pick up on something, I light a candle and hand it back to spirit with a prayer: "Spirit, I give this situation to you. If you would like for me to do anything with what I am seeing, please provide the opportunity for me to respectfully do so."

Can you think of a time when someone walked into your energetic space without your permission? How did it make you feel?

## Healthy Boundaries

Since we are examining spiritual ethics and boundaries, I would like to state that as a spiritual practitioner, you get to have your own healthy boundaries. This is not commonly talked about, so I wanted to mention it in order to empower you.

You do not need to work with every person who approaches you. For the most part, I do; however, on occasion I have been known to let someone know that I am not the healer for them. I do not need to explain myself any more than that. That is a healthy boundary, and healthy boundaries do not need to be justified. However, I will share with you that if I sense an individual has a harmful motive or wants me to "prove myself" as a practitioner, I do not engage. You see, for a believer, no proof is necessary, but for a doubter, no amount of proof is enough. It is not my job to convince another. It is my job to take care of myself so that I can show up for others. As long as I remain pure with loving intent and show up for those who request me, the rest falls into place. What are some of your healthy boundaries?

## Balanced Exchanges

Energetic exchange is something that must happen when doing any type of spiritual work. Whether you honor a bartering system or accept financial payment, balanced energy shows us that there is always compensation. With that being said, at times I will work with someone who cannot afford to pay me for what I do; I do this as an offering to spirit. Inevitably, the Universe will reward me in other ways.

I see spiritual gifts and energy as something that is worth a balanced exchange. This is the way it has been for centuries. Traditionally, when someone went to a shaman, they would bring the shaman gifts. When a traditional shaman dedicated their life to this practice for the tribe, the tribe took care of the shaman. We must take care of ourselves if we want to show up for others.

## STAGES OF SPIRITUAL GROWTH

I have a theory that each of us undergoes stages of spiritual growth. I have found that spiritual development is reflected in the patterns of development that exist in the physical realm. In this section, I will reflect on human development and then correlate it with spiritual development in order to better illustrate spiritual growth.

### Erikson's Stages of Human Development

While I was studying for my doctorate in leadership, I came across Erikson's eight stages of human development. This is a well-known theory within the medical field, the field of psychology, and the education field, and it even influenced my coursework since I was studying human nature. I'd like to share a recap of Erikson's eight stages of human development. Please note that the exact years and descriptions of these stages of development may differ slightly depending on the source.

- Stage 1: **Infancy** (birth to one year). In this stage of development, we trust that all of our needs will be taken care of.
- Stage 2: **Early Childhood** (ages one to three). This is the stage when we begin to understand independence and undertake some small tasks.
- Stage 3: **Play Age** (ages three to six). In this stage of development, we begin to understand boundaries.

- Stage 4: **School Age** (ages seven to eleven). In this stage of life, we develop self-confidence as well as feelings of sadness or inferiority when we don't succeed.

- Stage 5: **Adolescence** (ages twelve to eighteen). This is the stage when we begin to develop our personal identity and determine how we fit into society.

- Stage 6: **Early Adulthood** (ages nineteen to twenty-nine). In this period of life, we establish deeper intimacy in our relationships.

- Stage 7: **Middle Age** (ages thirty to sixty-four). In this stage of life, we focus and reflect on our contributions to society.

- Stage 8: **Old Age** (ages sixty-five plus). This is the stage of life when we try to make sense of it all.[11]

## My Stages of Human Development

Inspired by this biopsychosocial model, I developed my own understanding of five stages of human development. My stages of development were based on my knowledge of Erikson's theory; my personal experience; my family's background in theology; my understanding of spiritual development, which integrated both Christian theology and my Indigenous bloodline; and my doctoral studies. Here are the five stages of human development as I see them:

- Stage 1: **Infancy.** The first stage of development begins at birth and impacts us until age two. In this stage, a caretaker

11. Mcleod, "Erik Erikson's Stages of Psychological Development."

helps us with our basic needs; they feed us, bathe us, put us to sleep, etc.

• Stage 2: **Play Age.** The next stage of development is ages three to six. This stage includes a lot of growth as we learn how to take care of ourselves a little more. We may begin to tie our own shoes, dress ourselves, and ask for what we need.

• Stage 3: **Childhood.** From ages seven to eleven, we experience childhood. This stage is about learning and modifying behavior. We learn what is acceptable in our household and elsewhere.

• Stage 4: **Adolescence.** The next stage of development is ages twelve to seventeen. This stage allows us to develop our individuality and discover how to fit in with social groups.

• Stage 5: **Adulthood.** The final stage of development encompasses ages eighteen and up. We become responsible for who we are and how we interact with the world.

## The Stages of Spiritual Development

My theory of human development can easily be applied to spiritual development, although in the spiritual world, we do not necessarily develop within a set timeframe. The length of time it takes each of us to progress from one stage to another can vary; some people develop faster, and some develop slower. However, the primary focus during the stages of human development aligns with the stages of spiritual development, which is why I have included the general descriptors.

- Stage 1: **Infancy.** In this stage, caretakers help us with our basic needs. In this case, a caretaker may take the form of a spiritual guide, mentor, pastor, etc.

- Stage 2: **Play Age.** This stage encompasses a lot of development as we learn how to take care of ourselves a little more. We care for the spiritual self via meditation, study, and prayer, especially when we pray without being prompted to do so.

- Stage 3: **Childhood.** This stage focuses on behavior and what is acceptable for our path. We begin to have a deeper, more personal relationship with the Divine.

- Stage 4: **Adolescence.** This stage revolves around individuality and how we fit in with others. We learn who we are and which role(s) we hold within a spiritual group.

- Stage 5: **Adulthood.** This stage is about being responsible for who we are and how we interact with the world. At this stage, others may look up to us for our spiritual progress. At this point, it is important to reflect: *What is my responsibility to the Divine? What is my responsibility to my spiritual path? What is my responsibility to others?* When we reach spiritual adulthood, we understand the responsibilities of this stage of development. We know what it means to be a spiritual worker, a spiritual warrior, a shaman, and a shadow worker.

These stages of development can be applied to the emotional and mental realms as well. Unlike the physical realm, the spiritual, emotional, and mental realms do not adhere to a calendar year; they are more fluid. This means that while great strides can occur, great stagnation can occur also.

## BEING A SHAMANIC PRACTITIONER

Be aware that some people will look up to you because of the way that you perceive things. Shamans tend to have a different perspective on life and a different way of interacting with the world due to our animistic approach, our understanding that all is energy, and our desire for balance. Due to these concepts and many more, shamans walk differently within the world.

Some people will ask you to lead them. Be honest and humble when you do, always encouraging them to hear their own inner voice and solidify their personal connection to the Divine. From my perspective, the goal is to be there for them and to assist them in their own personal development. Think back to the spiritual development stages; when they are babies, attend to the baby. Always recognize that it is about the baby and not about you. When they grow up, they will require different forms of guidance. Be there for them. Remember that they are the next generation of spiritual practitioners. They are the next generation of leaders.

Being a shaman is a selfless act. We show up for another's growth. We show up for each other. That is the way of the shaman. Please take this understanding under advisement. At the end of your journey, may you be blessed because you have journeyed along with others. Dr. Scott Peck defines love as the ability to extend oneself for the growth and evolution of another.[12] I extend myself to and for you!

12. Peck, *The Road Less Traveled*, 15–17.

# PART II
# MEETING THE SHADOW

# BEGINNING THE JOURNEY

This is where we begin the journey. There are four stages to this process, each with their own chapter. Please spend some time with the chapters, taking a few days, a week, or another comfortable pace that allows you to fully engage in your shadow work. Each of the four chapters will flow in line with this process:

- A section on the spirit animal guide that works with that stage of the process
- A meditation, followed by journal prompts that expand upon the experience of the meditation
- The landscape explored in the meditation and its connections
- The time of day and season that correspond with this stage

- How to work with the medicine wheel, a direction, and an element for each stage
- One or more tools to work with that honor the stage and its associated spirit animal

## WORKING WITH ANIMAL TOTEMS AND SPIRIT ANIMALS

Animals come into our lives for a reason, a season, or a lifetime, much like we come in and out of each other's lives. When an animal comes in for a reason, it is here to show us how to move through a certain situation. If an animal comes in for a season, this animal will assist us for a period of time. When an animal comes in for a lifetime, it is referred to as an *animal totem* or *spirit animal*. My ancestors taught me this; they learned it from their ancestors, who learned it from their ancestors, and so on.

I am excited to share this section about spirit animal guides and totems with you. Animal guides and totems are an excellent and natural way to connect with the Divine. However, before we begin, I must be responsible for all the information I have gained, and I would like to share this sidenote with you: There is a particular sensitivity to cultural appropriation and the terminology *spirit animal* and *animal totem*. Some would suggest that this term is solely a Native American Indigenous concept. However, when I researched the origins of the terms *spirit animal* and *animal totem*, I found that there was no definitive origin for this terminology. The terms *spirit animal* and *animal totem* are typically associated with animals familiar to one's spirit, or they are used in a spiritual context, including shamanism—which is not solely a Native American Indigenous practice. With that being said, the word *totem* does have roots in the Ojibwa language.[13] Because of this, many individuals associate the concept of having a spirit animal or a totem animal with the Indigenous peoples of North America. Some even claim that Indigenous peoples coined these phrases and this concept; however, this concept is worldwide. The connection between the human race and the animal kingdom is a very natural one, and the human/animal connection can be found in legends and lore all over the world. While modern terminology may have roots in an Indigenous language, as in the case of *totem*, that does not mean the concept is strictly Indigenous.

This then raises the question "Can non-Indigenous people utilize the terms *spirit animal* and/or *totem animal*?" My position is that these terms and concepts are found worldwide, so anyone can utilize them. However, if you would like to be more careful with your wording, it would be more appropriate to state that you have a spirit animal rather than a totem animal. I am not that sensitive, so I continue to use these words interchangeably.

To directly attach this concept solely to Native Americans might at first sound like a compliment or a way of showing respect. However, I have a different opinion based on my lived experience—association with the spirit of an animal could lead to being perceived as less than human. My Navajo father was called a "savage," meaning less than human and more like an animal. Although my father rarely spoke of his time in boarding/residential schools, every now and then he would share. One day, he told me a story: When he was young, my father learned about these people called "savages." He was afraid of these savage people. One

---

13. *Merriam-Webster Dictionary Online*, "totem," accessed August 1, 2024, https://www.merriam-webster.com/dictionary/totem.

day, during recess, he went up to his friend and told him that he was afraid of the "savage" people.

His friend looked at him and said, "They were talking about us."

My father responded, "I am not a savage, I am Navajo."

And so it is. Although one might think the injustice in my father's story was that the colonized thinker was brainwashed to think that Navajo were savage—that the red body and the Indigenous, non-colonized individual were savage—the truth is that my dad was taught that he was savage. That is injustice. And that is my generational trauma right there.

What comes to mind when you read the word *savage*? For me, I think of the words *uncivilized*, *untamed*, and *unruly*. A savage is one who does not have a mind that can be tamed. My question is, tamed by what—or tamed by whom?

Back to my point: although current definitions of the terms *animal*, *spirit animal*, and *totem animal* view these terms and concepts in the adorning light of spirituality, this wasn't the case when my father was young and was directly referred to as an animal, as a savage. In the 1930s, when my father was born, the widespread colonized mindset was that humans were above animals, to such a degree that animals did not have a spirit nor a soul. I respect that conversations are now being had about cultural appropriation and appreciation; however, in my opinion, we are still at the early stages of these conversations. We still need to empathically understand what has happened instead of glossing over it. Much has been stripped from Indigenous people, and we shouldn't inadvertently cause more harm due to lack of historical understanding. I know this personally, as I am Indigenous.

However, even though I am Indigenous, I do not speak for all Indigenous people—I speak only for myself.

This is where I see the disconnect. The Indigenous people are the most current representation of all of our ancestors sitting in a circle. However, if you go back far enough into any race or culture, you will find representations of a tribal culture with deep connections to the animal kingdom. This traces back to the beginning of the human race. If you believe in evolution from a scientific point of view, you can see our connection to the animal kingdom; if you have a biblical point of view, you can find stories of animals speaking to us in the Garden of Eden. The human race has always been looking to the spirits of animals to express ourselves and our connections.

Animals play a significant role in all religions, cultures, legends, fairy tales, and lore. They are also an important part of language, to the extent that they often appear in popular phrases. In English, this includes sayings such as "He's as busy as a bee," "She is a workhorse," and "I am a night owl."

With this, I hope you find the liberty of self-expression and awareness as you read through the sections on spirit animals and totem animals. When we work with a particular animal or the spirit of an animal, we are learning from the way they move within the world. Do they fly near the heavens and observe the earth from a bird's-eye view? Do they stay grounded and walk among us? Do they gracefully slither along the earth? etc. Understanding an animal's movement and their position within the air and/or on the earth provides us with a deeper understanding of them, and in such, it allows them to have a deeper connection with us.

## The Animal Spirits in This Book

In this book, we will be working with animals that have a bad rap, just like the shadow does. These four "villainous," taboo animals have much to teach us. They will show up for us and assist in our shadow work.

### The Raven

Meet the raven, the mystical black bird that tends to show up in scary movies or within dark artistic expressions, including the artistic work of Edgar Allan Poe. The raven is known to rummage through trash or eat roadkill—not a pleasant sight for most people and cultures. With the iridescent coloring of its feathers, the raven appears very mysterious. Some see the raven as ominous, just like the shadow.

### The Snake

For many, the slithering snake was introduced as a creature of punishment. In the Bible, the snake represented the devil who tempted Eve in the Garden of Eden. Additionally, in Disney's classic *The Jungle Book*, the villain was a snake named Kaa. Kaa attempted to hypnotize and harm the main character, Mowgli. In many stories, it is common for the snake to slither into a dwelling as an unwanted guest.

### The Owl

The owl is a bird that is most active at night. Its flight is so silent that it is undetected until it chooses to strike. The owl has an almost alien face and can turn its head up to 270 degrees, which likely led to it being known as a harbinger of bad omens, including death. In many cultures, owls were believed to be messengers of evil witches and/or bad medicine people; they were believed to bring curses or bad medicine to those who heard them hoot. Nowadays, owls make appearances in scary movies to indicate that otherworldly forces are at play.

## The Wolf

The wolf is a villainous predator in many children's stories. In the story of Little Red Riding Hood, a wolf disguises itself as the little girl's grandmother in an attempt to eat her. In "The Three Little Pigs," a wolf tries to blow down the pigs' houses so it can eat them. Wolves have been villainized in many stories.

## Using These Animals in Shadow Work

Each of these four animals have been villainized. From an early age, we have been warned about these animals in children's stories, legends, and lore. As a result, many adults fear ravens, snakes, owls, and wolves. However, these four animals and their spirits are exactly what we need as we work to embrace the shadow side, for these spirits pay no mind to what others may think of them. These four animals have a bad rap—and so does the shadow. We will work with these spirit animals to uncover the mystical, magical, misunderstood shadow side.

The first step of shadow work is to recognize what is happening. Is an individual being reactive or proactive, and why? Until we keenly recognize what is occurring, we cannot address it. The raven is able to fly into the darkness of the void and bring out treasures—in this case, the truth. The raven asks questions. Its keenness helps us recognize the shadow. But what do we do once we recognize the shadow? That is the next step in the shamanic journey.

The second step is to diagnose the shadow. It needs to be acknowledged. This is where the snake comes in. The snake has an ability to clear away residual energy (in this case, the debris from old ways of thinking) in order to fully acknowledge the shadow within us. We may not completely understand the shadow at this point, but we see that it is real. The poison is the medicine, and the healing lies within the pain. Do we shed the old skin of the snake and become new? That is the choice each of us must make.

The third step is to understand the shadow, as scary as this might be. Which animal can provide insight into darkness? The owl. The owl has the ability to see what has been hidden and shares the truths that many would rather avoid. It understands why we are here. This can create feelings of vulnerability. Only when we face our greatest fears can we understand ourselves and our shadow self. But how can we make peace? How can we fully integrate our light and dark sides? This will be the focus of a later chapter.

The fourth step requires knowledge of, and personal respect for, the self. We must have a safe place to land. Here comes the wolf—the teacher with all four feet on the ground. This is the time to sense safety; we cannot process everything that we have been through until we feel safe. So, do not be threatened when you finally begin to feel. The wolf will accept you and your shadow.

The keenness of the raven will help us recognize the shadow. The diagnostic ability of the snake allows us to acknowledge the shadow. The insight of the owl helps us understand the shadow.

The knowing and teaching aspects of the wolf show us how to respect the shadow.

The next four chapters are dedicated to these animal spirit guides as we approach a very taboo topic: the shadow self. I encourage you to approach the shadow with curiosity and an inquisitive mind. Most of all, may we approach the shadow from a position of wonder.

## WORKING WITH THE INGRESS AND PORTAL MEDITATION AND THE PROMPTS

There are many ways to enter an altered state of consciousness, some of which were explored in chapter 3. The most organic way of entering an altered state of consciousness is through natural creativity, specifically artforms. Some people sing or play a drum to enter an altered state. Some dance, and others draw or paint. Ultimately, any form of artistic expression can take an individual into an altered state of consciousness, including storytelling or listening to a story. For this reason, I have provided a story (i.e., a guided meditation) to focus the mind on a certain landscape and experience. I strongly recommend that you have a journal with you throughout these sections of the book, as journal prompts will be provided for you and your work.

In each of the following chapters, the meditation falls under the title "Ingress and Portal" and is followed by a section titled "Journal Prompts." My husband wrote the Ingress and Portal sections; he has a deep understanding of storytelling and shared inspiration from his heart. Afterward, I included journal prompts that will assist with recording what was experienced during the meditation. To be clear, the Ingress and Portal sections are trance work, which others call *journey work* and some call *guided meditation*. All are three sides of the same triangle.

## WORKING WITH THE LANDSCAPES

Each landscape holds the spirit of that landscape within it. We experience different sensations in various landscapes. Some landscapes feel more comfortable to us; they have a familiarity to them, a sense of closeness. Others have an air of mystery about them, or they are very foreign to us, as though we have never encountered that particular landscape before. It is the same when we are working with the shadow and the landscape the shadow exists in. The shadow may hide in a landscape that seems familiar and mysterious, a place we are aware of but don't often frequent.

There are external landscapes within the world, and there are internal landscapes based on our experiences, thoughts, and emotions. Think of it like dreamwork: When you have a dream, it is within a landscape. This landscape holds clues and truths that the dreamer can reflect on in order to gain a better understanding of the dream. So it is with journey work and guided meditations—they provide broad strokes of a landscape for us to engage in. However, journey work and guided meditation should not be limited to only what I have provided. Please allow your internal counsellor to add to, change, or morph your internal landscape as you experience the guided meditations within this book.

As shared previously, each chapter includes a guided meditation. In each of these Ingress and Portal stories, please pay attention to the landscape. Work with your five senses to allow the landscape to come alive and speak to you. Additionally, note any emotions or thoughts that come up during the journey. Do not limit yourself to seeing only what the story shares with you; allow the landscape to provide deeper insights for a custom experience. For example, you may see something within the landscape that isn't provided in the written material. If you do, pay attention to it. It is your shadow's story and must be respected. Work with whatever comes up within you, as it will hold personal truths for you and your shadow.

## WORKING WITH THE TIME OF DAY AND THE SEASONS

There are four times of day: morning, noon, evening, and nighttime. Each of them has a different feeling about them. Each of them has a different light, and each of them casts a different shadow. In working with the times of the day, a person is able to embody these sensations through their own lived experience.

In the morning, many of us wake up after being asleep. The sun is rising over the horizon and fresh dew can be found on the ground. This is a time to rise, to stretch, to start anew. This is the time of daybreak and first light. The world is stirring, and the birds are singing. This is the time of new beginnings. The morning provides a time of recognition for the full day to come.

Noontime is a time of full light, as the sun is at its highest point in the sky. This is the time when it is hardest to find a shadow, but technically there is a shadow and, depending on the season and placement of the sun within the sky, a shadow can be found. The shadow is hidden at this time of day, so the shadow worker must search for it. The noontime can bring things into the light.

The evening is the time when many of us settle in and begin to relax. A full day has passed, and it is time to reflect on the course of the day. The sun is setting in the west, and we may spend time contemplating and processing the deeper meanings of our experiences. The evening brings us insights that can lead to understanding.

At night, the sun has moved out of visibility and the moonlight catches the eye. This is a very magical and mystical time of closure. Stars can be seen in the sky as the day's journey has come to an end; there is little, if anything, left to be done. At this point, we may feel a sense of accomplishment. Many of us lie down and rest. The night completes the cycle.

Similarly, there are four seasons in a year: spring, summer, autumn, and winter. Again, each season holds a different feeling and sensation, different light and different shadows. In working with this understanding, we are able to connect with the seasons on a deeper level.

Morning is to the day as spring is to the year. The earth is waking up and new seeds are beginning to grow. The freshness of the earth is nurtured by springtime's rainfall. The small animals that hunkered down for the winter are scurrying around and beginning to cultivate new life in the landscape. This is the time of new beginnings.

Noontime is to the day as summertime is to the year. It is a time of great sunshine and light. There is plenty of growth, and the earth is full of greenery and wonderful-smelling flowers. This is an exciting season, brimming with life force energy. We can utilize summertime to expand our consciousness and become more comfortable with life's experiences.

The evening is to the day as autumn is to the year. This is the time of great harvest—we can enjoy the fruits of our labor. The weather begins to change, and the days become shorter. The earth starts to fall asleep as the last leaves fall from deciduous trees. The breeze is a little crisper, and a winter chill can be felt in the air. We may begin to relax and accept the natural world as it is presented to us.

Night is to the day as winter is to the year. In winter, the nights are longer than the days. There is less movement within the animal kingdom and no growth on land. Most plants become dormant. A stillness, a quietness, can be experienced. A blanket of snow may cover the ground as the natural world falls into a deep sleep. And so it is within us: a time of quietness and deep reflection.

## WORKING WITH THE DIRECTIONS AND ELEMENTS

There are four different cardinal directions: east, south, west, and north. When facing different directions, I gain new perspectives. I can see things in a different light—and with a different shadow. The ability to perceive from different directions in order to take in the whole picture is important for a shaman who is working with the shadow.

There are also four elements: air, fire, water, and earth. These elements create everything, both seen and unseen, both tangible and intangible. When you connect to the four elements and work with them, you align yourself with the magic of creation as a co-creator. We are co-creators within our lives: we co-create with earth; we co-create with others; we co-create with the Divine and the Universe. The manifestation of the Universe is within you and is you; the manifestation of the Universe is within me and is me. We were created to be creators. When we step into our creativity, it is then that we begin to truly recognize the power of the Universe.

Working with the four elements might seem basic, yet it is a very powerful practice. The four elements make up all matter and are the foundation of science, medicine, and even philosophy. From the perspective of the natural world, the four elements are the cornerstones of life. They are essential for our existence, from the heat of the fireball in the sky that we call the sun, to the earth beneath us and its minerals within our bones, to the air that we breathe, to the water that we drink to sustain us.

From a spiritual perspective, we are able to manifest as we work with the elements and align the elements with the four stages of manifestation. The air element is the idea or thought we have (i.e., wanting to paint a picture, write a poem, start a project, etc.). The fire element is the action we take upon that idea or thought. The water element is the emotion we experience as we are manifesting (perhaps hope, joy, or anticipation), and the earth element is the final manifestation in the physical realm when the work is complete.

Within each chapter, we will return to the basics of life and of manifestation because who we are is reflected in what we do and how we do it. At times, we might get caught up in confusion about who we are and what we should do—we second-guess ourselves. We get caught up in the "what ifs" or say things like "I can't" or "It won't work." But these are imaginations. There is a basic truth: we are co-creators of our life, and we are here to create something. What we want to create and how we go about creating it reflects our authentic self.

When we return to the basics of life, we return to the understanding that we can do anything we put our mind to as long as we truly want it and have the discipline to take the steps to make it happen. Writing about this reminds me of when I was a child and could be anything that I wanted to be within my mind. Of course, there might be external extenuating circumstances that push back on our manifestations, but the possibilities are endless.

Don't write off any of your manifestation ideas until you have started trying them—in other words, don't stop before you've begun! To begin to manifest a goal, all you need to do is to focus on four things everyday: the four elements. When we connect with the four elements, we begin to learn (or remember) how to connect to the basics of life, how to continue to manifest our dreams, and how to utilize the keys to the Universe. We are here to co-create as an expression of the Divine that created us and that is within us. This is how to live a life with purpose.

In order to align with elemental energy, we first need to recognize it. We need to direct our attention to the elements within the experiences and landscapes we encounter. There is a deep wisdom within the landscape; it is one of the greatest teachers we have. Nature helps us understand life's flow and the dance between all things. The next time you step outside into the natural world, I invite you to look around and note each of the four elements within the landscape. How are they flowing together?

Here is an example of what this may look like.

*I step outside and direct my attention and focus to the natural world. The four elements begin to reveal their dynamics to me. The wind in the air moves and sings with the grass and the trees. The sunshine from above brings warmth to my skin. Later, rain from the heavens will cool the earth below. The trees provide shade from the sun and shelter from the rain. I acknowledge the elements and recognize how they dialogue together. I make myself a part of this dialogue.*

*Through this dialogue, I begin to understand the elements. The acknowledgment, or knowledge, moves from my head into my heart, and I begin to feel it and understand it on a deeper level: a heart-centered level. Now, I have become a part of the landscape. Now, I have found my place within the world. Now, I understand that the four elements are working together, and I am a part of them, and they are a part of me.*

*The more I understand, the more I am able to respect. The more I understand, the more I feel respected for the life that I have lived. Respect is a deep admiration for someone or something. Taking the time to understand something shows respect. Spending a moment with the natural world and the four elements showed me this quality.*

*I turn my head and look at a tree. It is no longer just a tree. Now, I wonder how long it has stood there and what life has happened around it and to it. Now, I respect the tree.*

The four elements are pure energy. They are the natural energies that create everything—including you, me, and the shadow. In this book, we will connect the four elements to the following concepts:

1. Recognition

2. Acknowledgment and communication

3. Understanding

4. Respect

These four concepts are the process to knowing thyself in all aspects, including the shadow. In chapters 5 through 8, we will walk through how to recognize each element, how to acknowledge and dialogue with each element, how to understand each element, and finally, how to respect each element.

When we work with nature to understand the shadow, we are able to gain a personalized experience of what each of these aspects mean to us personally and collectively in order to relate to the world around us. Moreover, it is important for a shadow worker to be able to get a complete picture using a variety of perspectives. These approaches will ensure shadow workers understand the full picture, the full experience, the full story. A multidimensional perspective honors everything, and everything becomes sacred.

## WORKING WITH A MEDICINE WHEEL

Broadly, medicine wheels have been around for ages in all tribes, not only Native American tribes (such as European tribes, African tribes, Australian tribes, the tribes within Asia, etc.). A medicine wheel can be assigned to a nation, a clan, a family, or an individual. Depending on the location, medicine wheels may differ from one another. Other things that can impact a medicine wheel are belief systems, cultural expressions, societal norms, what is available to a tribe, and how a person or tribe views the world around them.

A medicine wheel is a circle. Although the circle is a basic, simple shape, it represents so much. It is a shape that doesn't have a beginning nor an end. It is ever flowing with balance and harmony. Circles represent oneness and wholeness; they are encapsulating yet expansive. An example of this is when people congregate in a circle: There is no head of the table, so to speak. All are equally important. It creates a sense of fairness and visual equality within a group. Each person represents a position, even if they are opposing sides. Or consider a community sitting around a fire; they form a circle. Mankind has recognized this pattern since the beginning of time.

Circles represent the never-ending expression of life force. There are many examples of the circle within nature. On a macro level, we see circular spheres in the planets. On a micro level, we see circles within cells and atoms. Circles make up our world and bring us into a connected flow.

Just like circles, medicine wheels encapsulate energies and balance energies together. Hence, experiencing shadow work within the context of a medicine wheel is important to provide us with a sense of balance and equality, and to create a oneness/wholeness with our shadow. In this book, we will be working with a shadow medicine wheel in order to provide more continuity. In each chapter, we will fill in a segment of the medicine wheel. This medicine wheel will include concepts shared previously: an animal totem, a time of day, a season, a direction, and an element. As we move through the book, the shadow medicine wheel will be our road map, and it will keep us balanced and centered within a sacred circle.

## WORKING WITH TOOLS

Finally, each of the four stages of shadow work will include at least one tool that can assist in the journey. An explanation of how to work with the tool will be provided, as well as a personal example of working with these tools, simply to provide deeper insight as to the effectiveness of these tools. These will be very basic tools that a shamanic practitioner works with.

Some of the most basic tools that a shaman can work with are provided to us by Mother Earth. For example, the feather of a bird holds the knowledge of how to fly, how to soar, and how to slice through the air. This wisdom speaks to us if we allow it. With this wisdom, the tool starts to become even more sacred. To increase the sacred bond with a tool, take care of it and place it somewhere special. Work with tools like a musician works with their instrument. If we take care of our tools, they will take care of us—a symbiotic relationship. Some individuals even give their tools sacred names to increase their connection to them. The more we know the tools that we work with, the stronger our practice will be.

You can ask tools to come to you with a simple prayer. Request that the perfect tools come your way. Perhaps you will find a tool while taking a walk outside, purchase one from a local shop, create one, or have one handed to you by another practitioner. If you take something you have found within the natural world, I recommend doing so with respect. Leave an offering of some sort: a morsel of food, a splash of water, maybe even a coin. Respect the land by leaving a gift so there is equally exchanged energy.

Remember the concept of animism? Everything has a soul; all is energy; energy is sacred. Tools are an extension of us. The feather is working with us as much as we are working with it. In these moments, we are in alignment with the natural world. For a shaman, a tool is an extension of self—of spirit. A good rule of thumb is to always consider a tool an extension of self. Do so with a sense of respect in order to intensify the tool's impact.

Tools hold energy, and you may want to dedicate these tools to your sacred practice. This is up to you and your spirit. Sit with the sacred tools and grant them the space to speak. Get to know them. Reflect on how a shaman would understand their tools. The tool will say, "I am you, and you are me. We are connected in the way of the Universe. We are all one." I recommend this practice to any spiritual practitioner, artist, or even a craftsman or mechanic. Once we learn how to work *with* a tool, we have a deeper connection, and the tool and the individual work as one.

Sacred tools transcend the physical realm and can affect the emotional, mental, and spiritual planes. Just like the instrument played by a musician can transcend space and time, so it is with magical tools and the shaman who knows what they are doing. Each tool will move and work in different ways; the more time and energy we invest into our sacred tools, the more effectively they will work with us.

# 5

# APPROACHING THE SHADOW (THE RAVEN)

This is the first of four chapters that will assist you in becoming a shadow worker. Together, we approach this chapter with the sole intention of finding the shadow. Remember, in order to find the shadow, we must seek it with respect and acknowledge what it would like to say to us. It most likely holds a wisdom we haven't been able to recognize yet, though it may sound vaguely familiar. The ego, at times, protects us from hearing a truth or wisdom that we previously weren't ready for. But if you are reading this book, you are not looking for your shadow alone—your shadow is looking for you. Not to harm you, but to share deep inner wisdom that you are now ready to understand. If you have made it this far, you are ready to hear what your shadow wants to reveal to you.

This chapter is about working with the spirit of the raven and the keenness the raven holds in order to find shiny treasures along the way. To the raven, the shadow is a shiny treasure that will serve us well as we work toward self-awareness and self-knowledge. The raven has the ability to find deep truths and bring them to the surface so we can recognize them. While the raven has an uncanny way of communicating that may sound eerie at first, it ultimately helps us connect with and hear what the shadow would like to share with us at this point in the journey. In order to find the shadow and speak with the shadow, we work with the spirit of the raven. Let's begin.

## RAVEN ANIMAL TOTEM

There are many myths, legends, and lore about the spirit of the raven. In this section, we will cover a variety of attributes of ravens in order to connect to their energy. The first way to do this is to recognize basic attributes based on the raven's characteristics and how it moves in the world. Feel free to add any personal or experienced insights that you have to this description.

First, the raven is a bird that takes flight and has the ability to see the world from a bird's-eye view; hence, it sees the bigger picture. As the raven takes flight with the element of air, it aligns with the mental realm. Ravens are known to be highly intelligent: they have the ability to put puzzles together and to work with tools. Crows and ravens, which come from the corvid family as well as rooks, magpies, jays, and other powerful birds, are highly intelligent. Corvids have self-awareness. This was discovered when scientists gave these birds a mirror test.[14] Corvids have the

14. Prior, Schwarz, and Güntürkün, "Mirror-Induced Behavior in the Magpie."

ability to understand when they are looking at their own reflection versus another bird. Most animals are not able to distinguish their own reflection; they believe they are looking at another animal. This awareness is very important when it comes to locating and recognizing the shadow.

The raven is the largest of the corvid family, which provides it with great presence and strength. Looking at the jet black yet iridescent color of the raven's feathers, one can infer that this bird is not afraid to go into the darkness or the unknown. As ravens are the color of darkness, they can navigate the darkness of the void, or the unknown/unseen aspects of self. Their flight takes us outside of our current mental state and allows us to experience other aspects of our consciousness that are not always recognized. It is the raven's keen insight that helps us take the first step toward recognizing the shadow.

Ravens are known to be taboo within many cultures, just as it is with the shadow. This is not only because of the bird's coloring, but because they are carrion birds, which are birds that are known for their ability to consume decaying flesh. As strange as this may sound, in short, they love to recycle and consume what other animals will not touch. This is one of their attributes: the ability to transport the deceased or the fallen heroes to the next realm through death. This includes the death or passing of an old understanding of self in order to move to the next realm within the spiritual journey: the realm of wholeness. The ravens are perched on the pyre to assist in this transformation.

Keeping in mind that the spirit of the raven is taboo to many traditional Navajo people, I will share a story from outside of the Navajo Way out of respect for my tribal elders. Within the Norse lore, there are two main ravens: Hugin and Munin. These two ravens sit on the shoulders of Odin, the All-father. Each day, Hugin and Munin fly down to all of the worlds, and with their keen insight, they are able to recognize what is occurring. They then take this information and bring it back to Odin. Odin loves Hugin and Munin; they are known to be "thought" and "memory."

Working with this side of the raven energy, our thoughts and memories work with us to keenly recognize the shadow and possibly its origin. The shaman of this place is the spirit of the raven. Collect all of the information that is provided here, then add any additional knowledge and wisdom that you personally have about the raven. Allow this shaman to assist in the first step of this journey: recognizing the shadow. Additionally, as a shadow worker, you may want to keep your personal connection to the spirit of the raven in your thoughts as you make your way through this chapter.

## KEENNESS LEADS TO RECOGNITION

Under the raven, there is a moment of quiet, a moment of peace prior to a good death. A good death is one without regret, and a peaceful feeling comes with a life well lived. When we are facing our shadow, we are facing a certain type of death—a death of our old understanding of self. And in such, we are embracing a new consciousness. This way of death is a surrender to the unknown aspects of self and the awakening of the shadow.

The magical properties of the raven are many. The raven has the ability to fly into the shadows without fear. With its dark, iridescent wings, it almost blends into the darkness of the void that we are about to encounter. Within the void, the raven finds hidden treasures: buried truths and deeper wisdom. The raven seeks these treasures so we can begin to realize the truth within the shadow.

The raven may ask poignant questions in order to reveal the truth. The talkative nature of this magnificent bird will help us ease into shadow work. Ultimately, the raven will help us shift our consciousness. With its keen eyesight and the intelligent, purposeful way it moves through the world, the spirit of the raven assists us as we begin to recognize the shadow.

## INGRESS AND PORTAL

Now, it is time for journey work, otherwise known as *trance work* or *guided meditation*. I invite you to settle into an environment that is comfortable for you, one where you will not be disturbed so that the beautiful silhouette of your shadow feels safe enough to come forth. Light a candle or make a cup of tea if that helps you relax. Set your journal nearby so you are able to access it after completing your journey.

This is the organic part of working with the shadow. This is the time when we allow the shadow to speak to us individually and authentically. Working with the shadow is sacred work; you will be directed and guided by your truth and the truth of your personal shadow. The shadow's truth may be a truth that you haven't seen very clearly until now.

First, set sacred space for this work. Feel free to read this part aloud if you wish:

> I am creating a sacred space and a sacred time. I draw a circle around this space and time and declare it sacred. It is within this space that I am whole; I am loved; I am me. There is a reason that I have

found myself here. I am ready to meet my shadow, and I know that my shadow has led me here and is ready to meet me too. Being here confirms that I have made an agreement to meet my shadow in this holy, sacred space. I welcome the Divine as it has revealed itself to me to walk with me here. I welcome the spirit of the raven and its magical keenness to accompany me here. I welcome my shadow with great honor and respect. Be here with me now. And so it is!

With this statement, you allow the ego and assumptions to slowly drift away. You have created a safe space committed to curiosity and discovery. You are now in a sacred space and a sacred time.

Begin your breathwork. Inhale through the nose. Hold your breath, then exhale through the mouth. Continue to breathe in this manner for at least a minute or two. This moves you from a conscious state into a more relaxed, observant position.

*Breathe in this place. Breathe in the spring wet prairies. Notice the warming humidity of the prairie as it is drying in the morning sun. The storm clouds that passed last night are drifting east, billowing still, popcorn white in the blue sky of the morning sun. Breathe in the scent of loamy soil, steaming up from below the dewy stalks of the big, blue-stemmed grass that surrounds you on all sides as far as you can see. The beaded water on the tips of its blades casts glistening prisms of light across the prairie, beneath* the ever-climbing sun, as you face east. You do not see your shadow behind you. The whirling wings of a dragonfly catch your attention, and you sense its flight path. Breathe in the warming air as the great prairie gives up its inspiration to the climbing sun.

In the distance, a lone structure stands between the horizon and the prairie, and you begin to walk east toward it. The sun warms your face, relaxing you, and you spread your fingers wide, lightly touching the wet tips of the stalks as you pass. In this vast, open landscape of waist-high grass, you seek the shaman of this place, but you sense no other presence than your own as you wade through the grass, high stepping at times, toe to heel.

The structure—a scaffold—stands before you. Pine pole stilts jut up high, supporting a long, branch-woven bed. It is from here that suspended earthly bodies are surrendered, unburdened and unbound, to the sky to continue a journey where only the wind may carry their weight. Long feathers hang from each corner of the bed, and you crane your neck to focus on one in particular. The beating of wings behind you startles you! Whooshing, widespread black feathers cup the wind above outstretched talons. The great black bird alights atop the burial scaffold. It sits, head cocked, looking at you. Its gurgled croaks are interrupted by loud clicks of its beak, sounding like wood blocks being struck with bone. Three others gather on the scaffold, fluttering their wings and cawing as they jockey up and down for a *position to observe you from. Being four now, their presence overshadows your own.*

*Through the cawing and throated efforts come their words. As they look down on you from their macabre perch, the first one speaks. "The burial tree bears the branches that we will speak to you from."*

*The second, defiantly: "I am the one who knows what I have done and why."*

*Another angrily says, "I am not afraid of you."*

*The fourth: "The shadow is your wisdom keeper."*

*They then ask, "Do you hear these words?"*

*Understanding their nature, you are now able to listen.*

*Breathe in this place and return when needed. You carry the raven's spirit and this landscape within you now.*

Slowly move out of your meditative state and return to the space that you are in. Gently wiggle your fingers and toes as you return to your surroundings. Allow your state of consciousness to be present with your body.

## Journal Prompts

I invite you to reread the previous section while still in a relaxed state. With your journal next to you, reread each word. As you read, reference this section for complementary journal prompts, taking a moment to pause and journal about what you are experiencing.

As you "breathe in this place":

1. How does your physical body feel about this place?

2. Are there any emotions that are coming up for you?

3. Which thoughts cross your mind?

4. What are you sensing with your five senses? Describe any smells, any sounds that you hear, any sensations you feel as you touch the grass, etc.

5. Are you seeing or becoming aware of anything else within this landscape? If so, write it down.

As you stand before the scaffolding:

6. What are you experiencing, if anything, when you are standing before this pyre?

7. What are you experiencing with the four ravens? How do you feel? How do you perceive the four ravens? Write your thoughts down in as much detail as you wish.

8. The first raven said, "The burial tree bears the branches that we will speak to you from." What, if anything, does this mean to you? Or what do you think the raven meant by this statement?

9. The second raven said, "I am the one who knows what I have done and why." What, if anything, does this mean to you? Or what do you think the raven meant by this statement?

10. The third raven said, "I am not afraid of you." What, if anything, does this mean to you? Or what do you think the raven meant by this statement?

11. The fourth raven said, "The shadow is your wisdom keeper." What, if anything, did this mean to you? Or what do you think the raven meant by this statement?

12. The ravens then asked, "Do you hear these words?" How does this statement make you feel, or what does it make you think?

13. Sit with the ravens for a moment. Is there anything else that the ravens want to say to you? They may or may not speak to you with words.

14. If there is anything else that you experienced here, please write it down.

15. How are you doing?

Now, take a few moments to simply feel and experience whatever is coming up for you. Journal as much as you wish. The rest of this chapter will assist you in understanding your experience. Before you move on, take a deep breath and relax. Take a moment to care for yourself.

## THE LANDSCAPE

In the Ingress and Portal section, we found ourselves in a prairie, wet from a fresh rain the night before. As a landscape, prairies have a sense of openness and expansiveness. Within this prairie there were no trees to obstruct the view; hence, this was a place where nothing was hidden. Everything was out in the open. Additionally, we were able to see wide open space with no set path—this reminded us that we can form our own way.

As we breathed in this place, we inhaled fresh, spring air that opened up our senses to a brand-new day. As we looked around, we noticed the dew that graced the stems of the grass and understood that the earth was taking in a drink of water.

Amidst this landscape, we saw a pyre, a structure assembled for burning a sacrifice or a ritualistic rite to release a spirit back into the air. Pyres hold a sacred energy of release. Although the pyre lays someone to rest, it also births something new. Death takes a being from one state to another, and so does birth. To die in one world is to be born into another.

The prairie is a sacred landscape. I hope you felt it as you breathed in this place.

## TIME OF DAY AND SEASON OF RECOGNITION

No matter where you fall on the face of the earth, the sun will rise in the east. This is the dawn of a new day. This is the first light—a time of new beginnings and new adventures. The morning dew sparkles within the sunlight and wet dewdrops fall, quenching the world's thirst as all awakens. New thoughts and ideas form within the freshness of the natural world, and within the freshness of embarking of a new day. Yesterday is a memory, and today we create our truth.

The morning is also a time of recognition. With the spirit of the raven guiding us, the morning offers us a full day to understand what we are awakening to. At this point in the book, we are awakening to the idea of the shadow side. It doesn't need to be frightening, for we have a full day of light to examine what we discover. I am looking forward to remaining in this morning light with you. We have the full day ahead of us. Let's experience the excitement and anticipation together.

Morning and springtime are times of awakening and of freshness. Seeds are planted in the hopes of a good harvest. Birds and other animals may give birth to their young. The sun rises earlier and the daylight is longer. The earth awakens after a winter of slumber.

We are in the beginning stages of a new journey. This journey will teach us who we are, why we are, and what we are, including the shadow side.

## MEDICINE WHEEL: DIRECTION AND ELEMENT

It is time to begin creating and working with the shadow medicine wheel. Remember that the medicine wheel is divided into four parts, and in this chapter, we are focusing on the first of the four. I recommend drawing a blank medicine wheel in your journal or on another piece of paper. Here is what the blank medicine wheel will look like.

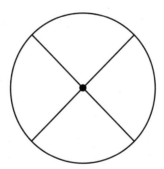

The blank medicine wheel

We begin with the right side of the circle because under the raven, we work with the east. The east represents the dawn of a new day. In many myths, legends, and lore, east is the direction of new beginnings. From a shamanic point of view, the east is very special. We greet it with thoughts and prayers during the morning light, giving thanks and gratitude to the direction for its insight.

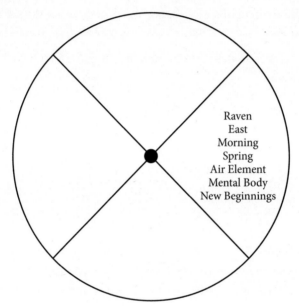

Raven
East
Morning
Spring
Air Element
Mental Body
New Beginnings

Working with the raven in the east

Here are recommendations for things to include in this section of your shadow medicine wheel:

- Write the word *east*.
- The animal that we are working with is the raven, so add this word as well, or draw or paste a picture of a raven within this section.
- Add any language around your impressions of the prairie.

- Since we are also working with the energy of the morning and of springtime, include these words or something else that represents these energies to you.
- The element that aligns with the east is air. Write or depict the element of air in this section of your shadow medicine wheel.
- Feel free to include your authentic touches in this first section.

The element of air aligns with the mental realm—the realm of thought. Is it natural to have a new thought or a new idea when we wake up in the morning. As we are becoming shadow workers, it makes sense to begin the journey here, in the east, with the energy of a new beginning in mind. As we reverently meet and greet the shadow, we give it respect by placing it in a respectable spot: the beginning. From this place, we withhold all assumptions of what the shadow is, and we approach it with curiosity. This is a sacred time. Here in the dawn of a new day, we welcome the dawn of a new perspective, the dawn of a new relationship.

## A TOOL

Under the raven, we can work with the tool of the feather. There are countless ways we can work with a feather, including feather magic. It is a sacred part of the winged ones that have a connection to the heavens above. Any feather that you have touched holds the knowledge of how to fly.

Feathers hold the magic of rising above. Feathers connect us to the sky above us, the bigger picture, the bird's-eye view. Is your heart as light as a feather? Can your heart see the bigger picture?

The feather asks the heart to rise above and see situations from a different perspective. Simply holding a feather and reflecting on a bird's-eye view can assist you in recognizing the shadow in a different way: one that is less personalized and more organic. The feather reminds us that we all have a shadow.

## Locating a Feather

If you do not already have a feather, you can ask a feather to come to you with a prayer. Simply request that a feather comes your way. A feather may appear while you take a walk in the natural world, or you may come across one available for purchase in a local shop. If you find or take something within the natural world, I recommend you do so with respect. Leave an offering of some sort: a morsel of food, a splash of water, maybe even a coin. What you leave is up to you; simply respect the land with a gift of equally exchanged energy.

When locating a feather, there is one thing to keep in mind. Make sure to check your local or regional laws, as some feathers are illegal to have. For example, it is illegal for a non-Indigenous person in North America to hold or carry an eagle feather; this law was created to protect these sacred birds.

Again, if you wish to purchase a sacred feather online, you can do so; just check with your local or regional wildlife service beforehand to ensure that your purchase falls under ethical standards. I will provide caution here: there are sellers who dye turkey feathers and pawn them off as sacred feathers, and there are other unethical practices in the industry. Simply be aware of this and let your magic guide your journey.

## Cord Cutting Using a Feather

As a shamanic practitioner, individuals come to me for help disconnecting from less-than-healthy situations and relationships. This modality is known as a cord-cutting ceremony.

In life, we connect with people, objects, and situations. We may physically, emotionally, mentally, and even spiritually connect with others. Additionally, the four bodies of existence (physical body, emotional body, mental body, and spiritual body) may connect to another's chakra(s) for several reasons. The root chakra may connect for a sense of survival; the sacral chakra may connect for pleasure and procreation; the solar plexus chakra may connect for a sense of establishing self in the world; the heart chakra may connect out of love and compassion; the throat chakra may connect out of a sense of self-expression (i.e., having someone to talk with); the third eye chakra may connect out of a sense of seeing or being seen; the crown chakra may connect due to a sense of spirituality.

Connecting in and of itself is a very natural occurrence, and it can have wonderful outcomes. However, at times, we may connect with an individual or a situation that is toxic or that has become toxic. There are so many examples of this. One example is a mother who will not allow her child to grow up and become independent out of fear of losing her identity as a parent. Another example is an individual who remains in a relationship long after the relationship has run its course. There are endless examples of toxic ties (or cords). When an individual is looking to create balanced relationships in their life, sometimes a cord-cutting ceremony is needed first. With a cord-cutting ceremony, the individual can disconnect from the imbalanced energy first, then rebuild healthier, balanced relationships.

Here is a shamanic perspective of working with a feather in cord-cutting ceremonies. A feather has a more defined side, like a blade, and a gentler side, like a paintbrush. This holds true for most mature feathers. This means that a feather can cut things away with one side, yet comfort and caress energies with the other. Since one side is sharp and the other side is soft, a feather is a tool that can cut through difficult situations and gently heal the severed connection directly afterward. For example, if someone is in a situation that is toxic and they are having a hard time disconnecting from the energetic exchange, a feather is able to slice through this situation like a surgical tool, precisely and definitively, in order to allow air and freedom to flow in. Then, the feather is able to soothe the severed edges with compassion in order to heal all involved.

A responsible healer or shaman will need credible training before attempting a cord-cutting ceremony. There is a responsibility to understand what can happen if the ceremony is not performed correctly: either there will be no outcome, or there will be an unlikely outcome, such as releasing energy prematurely and causing more difficulty within the relationship. I want to offer a personal example of a time when I went into a cord-cutting ceremony unprepared. My hope is that this allows you a better understanding of what occurs in a cord-cutting ceremony, and that it will dissuade you from getting involved in something without a fuller understanding of the situation. Please learn from my mishaps.

A dear friend came to me asking for help. She was in an unbalanced relationship, but she was so drawn to this relationship sexually. I wanted to assist my friend, and I wanted to release her from anything that could harm her, so I instinctively agreed to assist her from a spiritual perspective. In my defense, I was a young shaman at the time, and I was comfortable helping without further investigation. So, I decided to sever the unbalanced relationship between my friend and this other individual. Using my feather, I went full force and cut the ties between them, not recognizing the powerful effect that it would have on their overall relationship. You see, it worked. Sigh. I forgot to work with the other side of the feather to soothe the severs. That's the first thing that I didn't understand. The second thing I didn't understand was that there was more to this relationship than I initially understood.

Each relationship needs to be examined from many different perspectives. Relationships are not a simple link between two people; most relationships have multiple connections. From a shamanic point of view, we must look at relationships from the four bodies of existence: the physical, the emotional, the mental, and the spiritual. Personally, I work with the chakra system as well, and I consider the other areas of life that the relationship impacts. I pay attention to how a relationship connects to the individual's family system, friends, and the community. I also note a relationship's sexual and spiritual connections. The more seasoned I become, the more I learn and understand.

So, when I swiped my bladed feather to sever the unbalanced relationship between my friend and her lover, I only considered my friend's experience, and she wanted the relationship to stop. I didn't consider what connected the two of them in the first place. I didn't consider the bigger picture. There was a business relationship between the two; there was a friendship between the two—there was more than met my eye.

Within moments of the ceremony, my friend's lover called her on the phone and said, "What just happened? Is everything okay? Something feels different. What is going on?" My friend explained what had happened to him, and he responded, "You should have let me know. All I feel is pain and loss."

Wow! Needless to say, I learned a lesson and want to pass that lesson on to you. Be responsible and ethical when you work with spiritual tools. Wise people learn from others' mistakes—be wise.

Work with your feather as a bird would. Allow it to cut through the air as well as glide with grace. Connect with the feather as though it is a part of you so that it *becomes* a part of you. When I work with a feather, I envision the feather as me or as a part of me, just like my hand is simultaneously a part of me and is me. This is true of any craftsman; the tool becomes an extension of the self. So it is with magical tools. The tool and the self function as one. This is the way a seasoned shaman understands their tools: "I am you, and you are me." Everything is connected in the way of the Universe. All is energy. Tools hold energy, and as such, tools become an extension of who we are as a whole. Your feather is working with you as much as you are working with it—in alignment, and in balance with the natural world.

Feather work is not only for cord-cutting ceremonies. Over the years, I have learned a general approach to working with the feather. Think of a situation that you would like to gain clarity on. Maybe the situation has become dense or heavy. Visualize this situation in a bowling ball–sized orb right in front of you. Don't include any people in this visualization, only the energy that the situation is producing. Then, add color and weight to this visualized ball of energy. The color may correspond with how light or dark you sense the situation to be, and the weight may correspond with how light or heavy the situation makes you feel.

Next, pick up your feather. With the sharp side of your feather, slice through this energy multiple times, until the energy releases and begins to disperse. Then, take the soft side of your feather and gently calm the air and any leftover energy. Allow the feather to dance in the air in a calming, soothing manner.

This exercise can result in different experiences, depending on the situation. Most individuals will feel lighter or freer within their energetic field; some may feel a sense of release. This working will assist in moving dense energy and releasing stuck energy, like a magical spell. This is a wonderful way to work with a feather.

Go forth with the wisdom of the feather in your heart, mind, and spirit.

## SUMMARY

This was stage one of our four-stage process of shadow work. From a shamanic point of view, shadow work is done through the wisdom of the natural world. In this chapter, we worked with the spirit of the raven, whose keenness helped us begin to detect the shadow. Other connections included the time of day (the morning, as we are at the beginning of the journey) and the landscape (a vast, open prairie to widen our perspectives). The feather was introduced as a tool that we can wield to cut away old ties and begin anew. Knowing more of this world and its elements, you are now able to better listen to yourself, to the natural world, and to the voice of your shadow. Breathe in this place and return if and when you feel the call. You carry this chapter's wisdom within you now!

# RECOGNIZING THE SHADOW
# (THE SNAKE)

In this chapter, we will be acknowledging and diagnosing the shadow. This is the beginning of breaking the shadow down and understanding what it is and, possibly, where it came from. Remember, as we approach the shadow, we must release judgment of it. This doesn't mean that we abandon our discernment, just judgment. These two words can be synonymous with each other, so let me clarify what I mean. Within this text, the word *discernment* means to have a sharp perception of any given situation or thing, withholding the urge to categorize it as right or wrong, whereas the word *judgment* means to deem right or wrong, good or bad.

When we practice discernment, we do not imply that the shadow is good or bad. We must withhold judgment in order to truly understand it. You see, the shadow has already experienced judgment. If you approach the shadow with discernment and release judgment, it will approach you in the same way. If you are looking to blame or judge your shadow, it will blindly look to blame and judge you. We meet our shadow on equal footing.

The shadow holds a wisdom we haven't been able to fully understand previously. If you are still reading this book, there is a reason: your ego is now ready to learn and understand a truth or wisdom that you weren't ready for until now. The ability to look at the shadow with discernment is the ability to look at the world with discernment. The ability to examine without judgment is the ability to release judgment of yourself and others. This is a good characteristic to have within any healing modality, but especially so for a shadow worker.

In this chapter, we will work with the spirit of the snake, an animal that is just as taboo as the shadow in certain cultures and communities. We can work with the spirit of the snake to clear away old perceptions of the shadow and allow it to come forward in its truth. The climate of discernment is a very dry one—it needs to be dry in order to stir up the air of emotional pretenses and bring them into the light of day.

To the snake, your shadow may be held within an old story—an old skin. The spirit of the snake understands this impasse, as it is an inherent part of its being: snakes encompass birth and rebirth, shedding their old skin in order to embody the new. Thus, the snake is our guide within this landscape. With the assistance of the snake, we will see old stories in a new light. We will shed an old skin or who we were prior. We will practice discernment without judgment. We will approach the shadow with a fresh understanding and acknowledge it as a wisdom keeper.

## SNAKE ANIMAL TOTEM

In this section, we will cover a variety of attributes about the snake in order to connect to its energy. The first way to do this is to recognize basic attributes based on its characteristics and how it moves within the world.

The snake slithers along the surface of the earth. One of the main attributes of the snake is its ability to shed its skin in order to become new. This transformation process is aligned with the element of fire, which is a very active and activating element. When fire touches earth, earth is transformed. Likewise, transformational and transmutational energy is found within the snake.

Additionally, the snake is a reptile. Reptiles are ancient creatures, and many, including snakes, are known to be cold-blooded. This means that their internal temperature is dictated by the external environment—they are unable to generate their own body heat. One interpretation of this is that snakes are sensitive to their environment. This is a very strong tool when working with the shadow, as it is also sensitive to its environment. The shadow is not entirely internal; it is altered by the environments we have been in.

As with the raven, the snake is taboo in many cultures, including the Navajo Nation. Hence, I will share a traditional story from outside the Navajo Way out of respect for my tribal elders.

In the Christian Bible, there was a snake within the Garden of Eden, the first place of creation. In the Garden of Eden, Adam (the first man) and Eve (his wife) lived in harmony with everything. However, there was only one rule from God: they must not eat the fruit of the tree of the knowledge of good and evil. One day, a snake came to Eve and convinced her to eat the fruit from this tree. In many interpretations of this story, the snake represents the fallen angel, also known as Lucifer or Satan.

Yet, over the years, the snake has also become a figure of health and healing. The caduceus is a popular symbol that represents health, and it is often seen in the medical industry. As the medical field has proven, the venom of the ailment is always a part of the cure. While snakes carry venom, they also carry its antidote.

When looking at an image of the caduceus, you can clearly see the snakes.

The caduceus

So, how did snakes go from being a symbol of temptation to a symbol of diagnostics? The caduceus was frequently depicted in Greek and Roman mythology, though the symbol may date back to 3500 BCE.[15] Serpent worship and sun worship were two primal ways humanity built relationships with the gods and goddesses, and as such, these forms of worship sometimes overlapped. Ancient Egyptians believed that the sun flew across the heavens like a hawk, hence its association with wings. The sun was worshipped for its ability to create new life and provide healing. Snake or serpent worship was also tied to healing; for example, the goddess Isis was associated with health and healing, and one of the crowns she wore often had a snake on it. Over time, the connection between the sun, the snake, and health was represented in the Greek figure Hermes (Roman Mercury) and the caduceus he carried. Another Greek figure, Asclepius, was known as the god of medicine and carried a rod with one snake wound around it. Although Hermes was widely known as the messenger god, it was his caduceus that became associated with health and healing rather than Asclepius's rod. The caduceus was first used as a medical emblem in the sixteenth century, and it is a medical symbol still widely used today.[16]

Another interesting note about snakes is that some will rattle their tail in order to alert those in the vicinity of their presence. The rattle is a warning. As a shamanic practitioner who works with a rattle, I find this very curious. I work with a rattle to break up blocked energy and to clear away residual energy in order to observe and diagnose. Shaking and vibration are powerful tools. There is an ancient practice within the Navajo Nation that is not written about often, but it is a gift that I carry: I am a Hand Trembler. What does a Hand Trembler do? We diagnose energy

15. Wilson, "The Caduceus and Its Symbolism," 301.
16. Wilson, "The Caduceus and Its Symbolism," 301–3.

through the trembling we sense in our hand. In other modalities, healers might experience a tremble of the hand when they are sensing energy through it, which is a little different than my work as a Hand Trembler. The Navajo have a specific way of working with this modality—it is to diagnose energy. Hand Tremblers sense and feel the vibrations of energy, both blocked and unblocked. Blocked energy causes disease, whereas unblocked energy has a flow and freedom of movement and expression. Like the rattle of a snake, my vibration sends a message.

## DIAGNOSIS LEADS TO ACKNOWLEDGMENT

The shadow may be tainted by other people's projections of what is acceptable and what is not acceptable. When we feel ashamed of who we are, this can become part of the shadow as well. Clearly, projection comes from the external environment, not from within. Remember, the snake is cold-blooded, and it depends on the external environment to regulate itself internally. Likewise, we may look to a group to indicate what is acceptable and what is not. Unfortunately, shame is a sword that many groups wield in order to keep control of their members. Shame can cause an individual to reject natural parts of themselves in order to please others in an effort to feel a sense of belonging.

If parts of the shadow developed as a defense mechanism due to trauma or shame, then there is a primal consciousness that will override the conscious mind. This is the amygdala portion of the brain—the part of the brain that activates fight, flight, or freeze mode—also called the *reptilian brain* or the *lizard brain*. The reptilian brain overrides logical thought and launches us directly into survival mode. We need to visit this part of ourselves in order to diagnose this aspect of the shadow.

This is where the snake totem comes in. The rattle on the tail of a rattlesnake shakes up and clears away external debris and residual energy, allowing us to shed old beliefs. We may not completely understand the shadow or its motives at this point, but we can acknowledge that it is real, and we know that the poison is part of the medicine. What does not kill us makes us stronger, and healing lies within the pain. Are you ready to shed your old self, like the snake, and become new? This is the choice each of us must make.

## INGRESS AND PORTAL

Once again it is time for your journey work, otherwise known as *trance work* or *guided meditation*. I invite you to settle into an environment that is comfortable for you, one where you will not be disturbed so that the beautiful silhouette of your shadow feels safe enough to come forth. Light a candle or make a cup of tea if that helps you relax. Set your journal nearby so you are able to access it after completing your journey.

This is the organic part of working with the shadow. This is the time when we allow the shadow to speak to us individually and authentically. Working with the shadow is sacred work; you will be directed and guided by your truth and the truth of your personal shadow. The shadow's truth may be a truth that you haven't seen very clearly until now.

First, set sacred space for this working. Feel free to read this part aloud if you wish:

I am creating a sacred space and a sacred time. I draw a circle around this space and time and declare it sacred. It is within this space that I am whole; I am loved; I am me. There is a reason that I have found myself here. I am ready to acknowledge more of my shadow, and I know that my shadow has led me here and is ready to assist me. Being here confirms that I have made an agreement to meet my shadow in this holy, sacred space. I welcome the Divine as it has revealed itself to me to walk with me here. I welcome the spirit of the snake and its magical diagnostics to accompany me here. I welcome my shadow with great honor and respect. Be here with me now. And so it is!

With this statement, you allow the ego and assumptions to slowly drift away. You have created a safe space committed to curiosity and discovery. You are now in a sacred space and a sacred time.

Begin your breathwork. Inhale through the nose. Hold your breath, then exhale through the mouth. Continue to breathe in this manner for at least a minute or two. This moves you from a conscious state into a more relaxed, observant position.

*Breathe in this place. Oven-dry air devoid of moisture dries your nostrils with its heat. The air distorts the base of the monolithic table top mountains in the distance, like a mirage rising above the warp of the contorting heat.*

*The punishing sun bares directly down on the barren landscape from a cloudless blue sky, casting no shadows beneath its midday blaze. The strong scent of the blue junipers' waxy needles lies close to the shrub. Here and there, twisted, sand-blown trunks jut up from a fractured sandstone landscape. You catch the earthy tang of burning sage coming from the entrance of the slot canyon, a natural landscape carved by water.*

*Facing south, you walk into the arroyo. Soon, you are deep within its crevasse, carved by torrential downpours of proportions you struggle to understand. A narrow passage—once a rushing river—snakes through the waterworn sandstone walls, which extend far above your head. Were those swift waters to return at this point, you would not escape them.*

*The slot canyon narrows to a V-shaped point where you must place one foot in front of the other, hands touching either side of the canyon walls for balance. Ahead, you hear the rattle of the shaman a short distance away. You shoulder through a hairpin turn, back against the wall, when a gust of wind from above sends a blanket of sand and dust upon you. Blinded momentarily, your palms feeling for contour, you sidestep into an alcove within the arroyo, following the sound of the rattle.*

*As the rattle's songs crescendo, the air clears, revealing a coiled serpent directly in front of you, furiously warning you of its presence. It is covered with the dust and sand from the wind that just passed and takes on the hue of the stone it sits upon. It strikes out at you, touching the top of your hand, and you recoil in shock, frantically looking for the telltale marks of fangs on your hand. Your heart is pounding, and you are trapped with your back against the stone, facing the agitated reptile. It strikes at you and once again falls short of its mark.*

*As the snake slowly recoils, its eyes are clouded and ashy—it is blind at this moment. The rattle on the tip of its tail is now still. It begins to inhale deeply, air hissing through its nostrils as its ribs fill like the drawing of a bellows. Its forked tongue flicks up then down, sensing your presence as it exhales, once again hissing. It inhales a second time, splitting its ashy skin, which slides off and away as the serpent undulates to free itself.*

*Now, the snake sits anew before you. Beautifully colored, the telling gold diamond pattern is clearly visible down its brown-and-gray scaled back. Its throat, neck, and chest look as if girded by ivory-white plates, and the elongated pupils within its bright yellow irises clearly focus on you.*

*"Venom, adrenaline, medicine." It speaks to you in neither word nor thought.*

*Understanding more of the nature of the snake and the landscape, you are now able to listen.*

*Breathe in this place and return when needed. You carry the breadth of the landscape and your connection to the snake within you now.*

Slowly move out of your meditative state and return to the space that you are in. Gently wiggle your fingers and toes as you return to your surroundings. Allow your state of consciousness to be present with your body.

## Journal Prompts

I invite you to reread the previous section while still in a relaxed state. With your journal next to you, reread each word. As you read, reference this section for complementary journal prompts, taking a moment to pause and journal about what you are experiencing.

As you "breathe in this place":

1. How does your physical body feel about this place?
2. Are there any emotions that are coming up for you?
3. Which thoughts cross your mind?
4. What are you sensing with your five senses? Describe any smells, any sounds that you hear, any sensations you feel as you touch the grass, etc.
5. Are you seeing or becoming aware of anything else within this landscape? If so, write it down.

As you move into the arroyo:

6. What, if anything, do you experience while you are standing within the arroyo?

During the encounter with the snake:

7. When you finally approach the snake, how do you feel? What is your initial reaction?

8. How do you feel when the snake strikes you?

9. As you witness the snake in its state of blindness, how does that make you feel?

10. As you observe the snake shedding its skin, describe your feelings and observations.

11. After the snake has shed its skin, what do you experience, think, and feel?

12. The snake shares a sentiment with you: "Venom, adrenaline, medicine." What do you think it is trying to relay to you? What do you understand at this point?

13. Take a moment to sit with the snake. Does it share anything else with you?

14. Watch the snake. Does it move or do anything else? If so, write that information down, as it could hold meaning for you personally.

Now, take a few moments to simply feel and experience whatever is coming up for you. Journal as much as you wish. The rest of this chapter will assist you in understanding your experience. Before you move on, take a deep breath and relax. Take a moment to care for yourself.

## THE LANDSCAPE

In this chapter's Ingress and Portal section, we found ourselves in the dry desert. The heat rose above the earth in iridescent waves that distorted our vision for a moment. This heat dried our nostrils and reminded us we were in a sunbaked landscape. And, since we were standing under the heat of the midday sun, it was difficult to find any shadow here. Do not let this fool you—the shadow was present.

We walked into an arroyo, which is created by torrential downpours. This is significant, as torrential downpours may have metaphorically occurred in life as well. Sometimes, when certain events take place, we become overwhelmed and feel a burst of emotional flooding. When we experience intense, possibly traumatic situations, they carve out a space within the psyche, now left with little or no growth. It makes sense that a part of the shadow would dwell in such a place within us.

When the wind kicked up the dust, our eyesight was taken from us. So, we listened carefully for any noises that drew us in and followed the arroyo's crevices with our hands and our feet. We were working with the senses. This is true of working with the shadow too: we must release our dependency on sight and what it can show us, instead sensing the landscape with our senses of hearing, taste, touch, and smell. Through this work, we embody the shaman.

## TIME OF DAY AND SEASON OF ACKNOWLEDGMENT

At noontime, we are able to see things in a bright light. All is fully illuminated; nothing can be ignored at high noon. As the sun sits in its highest point in the sky, there seem to be no shadows cast, but there are other elements at play here. The winds may kick up a sandstorm to distort or distract the vision of a seeker, for example. Dust that is stirred up makes it very difficult to see. Hence, we needed to move through this time of day with our other senses, as our eyesight could fool us. Be aware of all other elements, as the shadow will want you to be dedicated to the journey in order to prove yourself. If the shadow finds you unworthy of understanding it, it will not reveal itself to you, even at the brightest time of day.

This is the time of acknowledgment. This is the season of summer, when daylight is the longest. We have more light and thus more opportunities to see the shadow, and as such, it is time to acknowledge the shadow.

## MEDICINE WHEEL: DIRECTION AND ELEMENT

Now it is time to continue to create and work with the shadow medicine wheel. Remember that the medicine wheel is divided into four parts; this is the second part of four.

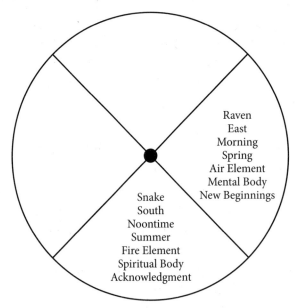

Raven
East
Morning
Spring
Air Element
Mental Body
New Beginnings

Snake
South
Noontime
Summer
Fire Element
Spiritual Body
Acknowledgment

Working with the snake in the south

We continue on in a sunwise (clockwise) direction to the bottom of the circle. While working with the wisdom of the snake, we work in the south. In many myths, legends, and lore, the south is the direction of growth and activity. From a shamanic point of view, the south is a very special place that holds the elements of fire and spirit. This is a direction of development and action.

Here are recommendations for things to include in this section of your shadow medicine wheel:

- Write the word *south*.
- The animal that we are working with is the snake. Add this word as well, or draw or paste a picture of a snake within this section.
- Add any language around your impressions of the desert or this landscape.
- Since we are working with the noontime energy and the energy of the summer, include these words or something else that represents these energies to you.
- The element that aligns with the south is fire. Add the word *fire* or another representation of fire that your creative side would like to include.
- Feel free to include your authentic touches in this section.

As stated previously, the element that aligns with the south is the element of fire. Fire aligns with the spiritual realm. When I read the words *spiritual realm*, I think of a spirited person. It is natural that spirited individuals are active, social, and fiery human beings. Within the spiritual realm, there is the concept of purification through fire. There is also anointment through fire.

Additionally, fire is found in most, if not all, spiritual practices as the flame of a candle. As a shaman, I was taught that the flame of the fire is alive and seen in all realms of existence. That is why it is so intense and powerful.

As we continue with our shadow work, it makes sense to continue the journey here, in the south, with the element of fire and the spiritual realm. As we begin to acknowledge the shadow, we can see its integrity holding the place of the south within the medicine wheel.

## A TOOL

Under the snake, we work with the rattle. The rattle has the ability to move energy within a given space; it shakes things up, moving the air and the energy. All is energy. When energy is stagnant or blocked, it causes discomfort and/or disease. This is not a philosophy; this is physics. Hence, a shadow worker needs to understand how to move energy, because the shadow is energy. Most likely, it is blocked energy. When energy has been silenced or told not to express itself, this can become harmful, blocked energy. A shadow worker needs to understand this and create a space where energy is safe and respected for what it is.

Knowing how to unblock energy is essential. Whether energy is blocked physically, emotionally, mentally, or spiritually, the same tool is needed: a sacred rattle. Here are the basic concepts behind this healing modality:

1. All is energy.
2. Energy seeks its freedom. Stagnant energy causes disease.

3. Freedom comes from movement.

4. Movement occurs via anything that oscillates.

Although a sacred rattle is within the physical realm, its movement can affect all four realms (physical, emotional, mental, and spiritual). The shaking of a rattle begins to stir up dense, stagnant energy, releasing it and preventing it from attaching to anything. Thus, stirring up, shaking up, and breaking up energy with a sacred rattle allows energy to find freedom.

Although I was able to spell this concept out in four basic steps, it is a very powerful understanding for any healer. We can see the benefits of moving energy in many fields. In physical therapy, the act of moving the body in a certain fashion allows energy to shift, creating a sense of release and a healthier flow of energy. In talk therapy, which can benefit us emotionally and mentally, talking and the movement of the voice box may start breaking up old energy, allowing for the freedom of movement and energy flow. Additionally, in many alternative healing modalities, there is a movement aspect that allows for the relaxation or release of old energy in order to find or establish a new movement of energetic expression. I've examined dozens of different healing modalities, and this four-step concept seems to be universal. Think about a healing modality that you know. Does this four-step concept align with your chosen healing modality? I invite you to explore other healing modalities that integrate this four-step concept, as they could be valuable additions to your toolbox.

Now, let's return to the idea of exploring movement using the rattle—the tail of the shaman snake. The first step is to acquire a rattle. Feel free to be creative here! You can purchase a sacred rattle or make one. For example, I found my sacred rattle during a visit to a local music store. I also have a rattle gifted to me by another medicine person. Objects within the natural world could serve as a rattle, such as a dried gourd. A rattle could even be crafted with items found around the home; I've had individuals tell me that they created their sacred rattle with a small container and some uncooked rice or beans. Regardless, when they shake it, it releases energy. As long as something creates a rattling sound, it can be a rattle.

Once you have a rattle, make it sacred. There are a number of different ways to make a magical tool sacred: meditate with it, sit with it, care for it. Place it under the midday sun just like a snake would bask under the midday sun. If there is a space to draw on the rattle, draw a snake so that it can be imbued with the spirit of the snake's tail. Remember to take care of your magical tools; you get to decide who can touch your sacred tools and who cannot.

The first time that I dedicated my rattle as sacred, I shook it around the outskirts of my body. I didn't need this to be part of a ritual or drawn-out prayer; I simply shook the rattle about two to three inches away from my physical form. Immediately, I felt a shift and release, sort of like I had just gotten a massage. Try it for yourself! I am sure you will feel something, as there will be energetic movement. The body responds very quickly to the sensation of energetic movement.

The more I worked with my rattle, the more it helped me discover. Working with magical tools allows them to become an extension of ourselves. I have a story I would like to share with you. Once, a man came to me with sciatica in his left leg. I addressed the lack of energy flow within his body from a shamanic point of view. He laid upon my healing table, and I set sacred space and shook the rattle around him, never touching his physical body. I visualized his spiritual body about eighteen inches above his physical body and shook the rattle to break up any blocked energy in this area. Next, I visualized his mental body (which I perceived as about twelve inches above the physical body) and shook the rattle. Then, I visualized his emotional body about six inches above the physical body and shook the rattle to clear away any blockages that his emotional body held. It was at this point I felt a deep sorrow within me, and the man began to move around. It was as though I stirred up something within his emotional body.

At this point, I focused on the man's emotional body and began to gently ask him questions. I released my ego and simply worked with the energy that was presenting itself. This is what we need to do as shadow workers: release the ego and allow the energy to express itself to us. Because the man was experiencing pain on his left side, I decided to focus on female energy. An old modality taught me that the left side represents female energy and the right side represents male energy. This wisdom returned to me for a reason, so I decided to ask basic questions about feminine energy within his life, starting with his mother.

When I asked about his mother, the man told me that his mom passed away unexpectedly right in front of him. He told me that he never cried about it and held the emotions within himself. He began to cry and release in the sacred space that spirit helped me to create. I shook the rattle to release the tears he didn't know how to express. It was an intense moment.

After the man finished the healing session, he got up from the table and walked out of the room without sciatica. Years later, he told me that he hadn't had sciatica pain since. The rattle is powerful.

## SUMMARY

This was stage two of our four-stage process of shadow work. In this chapter, we worked with the spirit of the snake, whose ability to break up energy, remove debris, and shed old skin helps us acknowledge the shadow, including where it comes from and how it behaves. Other connections included the time of day (the heat of high noon, when shadows are hard to find) and the landscape (a desert with an arroyo that was created by torrential downpours, representing how the past shapes the present). We worked with the rattle to break up old patterns. As we allowed the dust to settle, we began to shed old skin and old beliefs about the shadow. We acknowledged it for what it truly is: a part of us. Knowing more of this natural world with the natural elements, you are now able to listen. Breathe in this place, and return if and when you feel the call. You carry this chapter's wisdom within you now!

# UNDERSTANDING
# THE SHADOW
# (THE OWL)

In this chapter, we will seek insights that lead to further understanding of the shadow. Together, we move into this chapter with the sole intention of gaining insight we wouldn't have otherwise—insight that can only come when we release the ego and let go of old emotions for a moment. In this chapter, we practice the art of being an "observer," a neutral position that can lead to deeper understanding of the shadow. This process is just like meeting someone for the first time: we give the stranger space and time to tell us who they are so that we can understand them.

Remember, as we approach the shadow, we release judgment of it, approaching it with curiosity and an open heart and mind. The shadow holds a wisdom that you weren't able to fully understand until now. If you have made it this far, you are in a space and time when you are able to better understand yourself, without the ego or previous judgments.

This work is assisted by the spirit of the owl, another animal that is just as taboo as the shadow in certain communities. Most owls are nocturnal, meaning they are awake and active at night. In many cultures, legends, and lore, nocturnal species have a direct correlation to darkness. Darkness frightens many people; because we are unable to see clearly in the dark, the fear of being blindsided is present. However, if an owl reveals itself to you, it saw you first and is allowing you to see it. So, let us work with the spirit of the owl and allow it to come forward in its truth and wisdom.

## OWL ANIMAL TOTEM

In this section, we will cover a variety of attributes of the owl in order to connect with its energy. The first way to do this is to recognize the owl's characteristics and how it moves within the world.

The owl is a bird that takes flight and has the ability to see the world from a bird's-eye view. But unlike the raven, the owl has nocturnal sight: the ability to see clearly in dark spaces. Additionally, the flight of an owl is quiet due to the shape of its feathers and wings—you will not hear an owl unless it wants you to know that it is there. This ability serves the owl in its hunt for small prey and fish. Their sight and silent flight make owls incredible hunters. These are some of the owl's strongest qualities. The quiet flight of the owl teaches us how to approach the shadow without frightening it. The owl also allows us to look deeply at the shadow, as its ability to see into the darkness provides us with increased energy in the third eye chakra. An activated third eye will lead us to insight that we might not have had otherwise.

Owls are found all over the globe, excluding the polar caps and some remote islands. Hence, their ability to adapt to multiple environments is another wonderful quality for us to work with. Owls are also widely known for their ability to swivel their heads up to 270 degrees; this attribute provides us with a larger lay of the land. The talons of an owl are razor sharp and are large in size compared to the rest of its body; this allows the owl to grasp large objects and cut through dense shells in order to expose the truth within whatever it found.

In numerous cultures, the owl is seen as the harbinger of death. There are many Native American tribes that believe that if you see an owl, death is around—either the person who saw the owl or a loved one will move from the day of life to the quiet death of night. However, even though some perceive the owl as taboo, others see it as a majestic omen, even a message from beyond the grave. The owl can help us connect with loved ones on the other side of the veil, if we so desire. This connection to the ancestors is key within shadow work, as some shadows are passed down from one generation to another. Understanding where we come from is a valuable insight.

Since the spirit of the owl is taboo to many traditional Navajo people, I will share a story from outside the Navajo Way out of respect for my tribal elders. In Greek mythology, Athena was known to be a warrior goddess who had an owl as a companion. Athena was very powerful and very wise—she provided great counsel to those who sought it. It was said that Athena's owl would sit upon her shoulder to reveal truths to her.

Similarly, my shadow will sit upon my shoulder and whisper truths to me. These are truths that my light side—my happy side, my optimistic side—may want to hide from my consciousness, such as "Not everyone holds good intentions," "Some people are only out for themselves," and "Not everyone wants to grow and become the best version of themselves." These truths are difficult for my light side to understand, as I wish everyone a blessed life full of love, well-being, and authenticity. However, there are those who believe a blessed life means having millions of dollars, watching their enemies fail, and always getting more, more, more. Being blessed is defined situationally and subjectively. My shadow assists me in understanding these truths in order to keep me balanced—not naïve. My shadow brings me the hard truths I might not want to see.

## INSIGHT LEADS TO UNDERSTANDING

As scary as it might be, we need to understand the shadow so that we can grow. Which animal totem can help us peer into the darkness? The owl. The owl has the ability to see what has been hidden and the wherewithal to understand those hidden truths. This can cause us to feel vulnerable. We may ask ourselves, *Who am I? What have I experienced, and why am I here?* Only when we face our greatest fears can we understand ourselves and our shadow self. But how can we make peace? How can we fully integrate our light and dark sides?

It is here that we return to the discussion of trauma, dissociation, and triggers that began in chapter 2. In that chapter, I noted that the shadow can be created during traumatic times, and some of those times can be passed down from generation to generation. This is historical trauma. Additionally, I spoke about dissociation, when consciousness disconnects from the physical body and the current situation. This happens when the conscious mind is looking for a way to avoid something, distract us, or numb us to a situation. Sometimes this happens when we get bad or life-changing news; it may take time to fully digest. That is totally normal. In these moments, the mind may dissociate. Some call this denial within a grief cycle. However, we are focusing on dissociation as a response to a traumatic experience or a trigger that was instilled by a traumatic event. Again, this event or trauma may have been passed down within the family tree. If we pay attention, dissociation and triggers have something to teach us.

When we dissociate, the owl notes what is present and relevant within a situation—the owl sees what we are unable to see at the time. Thus, the owl becomes a storehouse of insight, which will lead to wisdom. When we approach the spirit of the owl, we must do so from the position of a student. The owl may work its medicine by asking us to lose the ego and our sense of judgment, for they are not serving us well. The owl may ask us to let go of the emotional state we were in when the trauma occurred in order for us to see things clearly. The spirit of the owl may even invite us to become disembodied, dissociated, and disillusioned so we can continue the natural cycle of healing. In order to complete the trauma cycle, we need to begin where we left off. However, this time we know that we are being watched over—we are safe.

The path of a shaman is not easy. We earn the medicine (the wisdom) that we carry. We earn it through life's difficult times and the dark night of the soul. The dark night of the soul is a very hard time in life that we must move through. Perhaps we have suffered a significant loss and can't seem to move forward, or we have disconnected from others. Whenever we find ourselves in a dark time, we can remember the spirit of the owl. With the owl's assistance, we are able to find the hidden gems in dark times and harvest the wisdom that we carry with our shadow, collectively and unified. I am not a shaman because my life was easy. I am a shaman because I became a student of life, and I continue to learn what life has to teach me. The owl is my guide.

## INGRESS AND PORTAL

I invite you to settle into an environment that is comfortable for you, one where you will not be disturbed so that the beautiful silhouette of your shadow feels safe enough to come forth. Light a candle or make a cup of tea if that helps you relax. Set your journal nearby so you are able to access it after completing your journey.

This is the organic part of working with the shadow. This is the time when we allow the shadow to speak to us individually and authentically. Working with the shadow is sacred work; you will be directed and guided by your truth and the truth of your personal shadow. The shadow's truth may be a truth that you haven't seen very clearly until now.

First, set sacred space for this working. Feel free to read this part aloud if you wish:

> I am creating a sacred space and a sacred time. I draw a circle around this space and time and declare it sacred. It is within this space that I am whole; I am loved; I am me. There is a reason that I have

found myself here. I am ready to better understand my shadow, and I know that my shadow has led me here and is ready to reveal more understanding to me. Being here confirms that I have made an agreement to understand my shadow in this holy, sacred space. I welcome the Divine as it has revealed itself to me to walk with me here. I welcome the spirit of the owl, with its insights that will lead me to further understanding, to accompany me here. I welcome my shadow with great honor and respect. Be here with me now. And so it is!

With this statement, you allow the ego and assumptions to slowly drift away. You have created a safe space committed to curiosity and discovery. You are now in a sacred space and a sacred time.

Begin your breathwork. Inhale through the nose. Hold your breath, then exhale through the mouth. Continue to breathe in this manner for at least a minute or two. This moves you from a conscious state into a more relaxed, observant position.

*Breathe in this place. Breathe in the water's cool vapors that swirl in the air. The air is moist, cool, and humid, cascading down upon you in misty airborne waves from the waterfall far above. You can both smell and taste the mist in your inhalation. The humidity forms droplets on the fine hairs of your arms and on the fine hairs of the emerald-green moss that clings to every stone. The moisture beads upon the shoot of the fern*

that clutches the bedrock that forms the waterfall—
fractured bedrock set ajar eons ago.

The vibration of the water's course is felt even
within the wet stone slab that you stand upon. Were
you to speak, the discernment of your words would
require effort. Your presence as a visitor here is
dwarfed by the volume of water rapidly sheeting over
the ledge above, falling white and dashing relentlessly
on the smooth boulders below. A rainbow forms within
the rays of the setting sun that floods the ravine with
its fading light. Turning west, you walk in the direction
of that setting sun, seeking the shaman of this place.

The game trail that you follow away from the
waterfall winds with purpose through the forested
bank beside the water. A trail worn by countless footfalls of hoof and paw, it meanders around tree trunks
and boulders, becoming increasingly difficult to discern in the lengthening autumn shadows.

Straining to see, ego abandons you as you wander off the trail here and there. You backtrack after
blindly veering off one of the many hidden turns that
you failed to see—a trick of the light. The pink tinge
of twilight gives you pause as you look up from the
trail, eyes dilating as you change your focus from
near to far. You marvel at the golden rays of the setting sun through a clearing before you. This evening
will bring no moon, and the shadows are dominant
as you struggle to see the path in the fading light of
the setting sun.

*In a few short paces, you are standing on a pebbled beach exposed by the ebbing tide. The smells of kelp and brine fill your nostrils as you clear the forest's ravine. Great snags of driftwood that form ghostly specters in a bay of receding water now seem sentient, with outstretched arms. Checking your footing on the slick pebbles, you walk upon the tidal plane until you stand before one of the colossal snags. Worn smooth and waterlogged, the skeleton of a once-majestic conifer is prostrate. It easily stretches twenty paces in either direction, and you cannot see over or beyond the girth of its trunk even though it lies securely anchored in the silt of the tide, flattened by its tremendous weight. You ponder what the tree witnessed when it stood a century ago. Its lifetime spanned countless generations that formed the tree of your own ancestors, ancestors now dimmed by time and distance when, green-needled and evergreen, this tree lived.*

*You instinctively walk toward the flare of gnarled roots at the far end of the immense trunk, inspecting the patterns of winding wood that meander out and away from the once-rooted stump. A glimmer from one of the roots catches your eye and you lean forward to inspect it in the dim autumn light. Embedded in the root is a multifaceted stone, held in place by years of growth. The touch of a finger reveals it was loosely held in place by the soft wood. With its weight in your palm, you run your thumb over the sharp edges of the stone's symmetry, exploring the flat faces of its geometric structure. It is clearly a magical crystal.*

*Pocketing your prize, you turn to leave, but the silhouette of the owl now perched on a broken bough is before you. The owl silently arrived behind you while you were distracted. It has come for the feast afforded by the ebbing tide.*

*As you walk toward the owl's silhouette, its head swivels to the right. Then, it turns its gaze upon you, its great talons tacking into the soft wood on which it is perched. It says, "Release your ego, your justified righteousness, your judgment and shame, or I will fly away."*

*You slow your steps as you continue to approach. The owl adjusts its footing upon the wood as its head swivels to the left, once again staring directly at you. It says, "Release your emotions of love and hate. Both are blinding. Bias must be abandoned, or I will fly away."*

*Disillusioned, you now stand before the owl. Disembodied from your ego and your emotions, you stand within the glare of its attentive eyes. Your own eyes try to focus in the failing light. The night hawk has come for the ebbing tide's exposure. It says, "Now, in the absence of light, you seek with clear vision."*

*Now that you understand the nature of this landscape and the spirit of the owl, you are able to listen.*

*Breathe in this place and return when needed. You carry the spirit of this place within you.*

Slowly move out of your meditative state and return to the space that you are in. Gently wiggle your fingers and toes as you return to your surroundings. Allow your state of consciousness to be present with your body.

## Journal Prompts

I invite you to reread the previous section while still in a relaxed state. With your journal next to you, reread each word. As you read, reference this section for complementary journal prompts, taking a moment to pause and journal about what you are experiencing.

As you "breathe in this place":

1. How does your physical body feel about this place? Describe the sensations in as much detail as possible.

2. Are there any emotions that are coming up for you?

3. Which thoughts cross your mind?

4. What are you sensing with your five senses? Describe any smells, any sounds that you hear, any sensations you feel as you touch the grass, etc.

   - When you are at the waterfall, describe the experience.
   - When you are wandering down the path, describe the experience.
   - When you find the pebbled beach, describe the experience.

5. Are you seeing or becoming aware of anything else within this landscape? If so, write it down.

As you stand in front of the skeleton of a tree:

6. What are you experiencing, if anything, while you are standing in front of this great tree? I invite you to stand there quietly for a moment. Is there anything that you are sensing? Write it down in as much detail as possible.

When you find the crystal:

7. What do you sense? What is your initial reaction?
8. Describe the crystal (i.e., shape, weight, texture, color).
9. Look around for a moment. Are there any more crystals that are calling to you? If so, pick them up and describe them. If not, that is perfectly fine.

During the encounter with the owl:

10. When you finally see the owl, how do you feel? What is your initial reaction? Does it change as you spend more time with the owl?
11. How do you feel when the owl asks you to release your ego? What about when it asks you to release justified righteousness, judgment, and shame?
12. How do you feel when the owl asks you to release your emotional stance? What about when it stated that both love and hate can blind us?
13. The owl said, "You seek in the absences of light with clear vision." Write down what this means to you in full detail.
14. Take a moment to sit with the owl. Does it share anything else with you? If so, what?

15. Watch the owl. Does it move or do anything else? Write this down, for it could hold meaning for you personally.

Now, take a few moments to simply feel and experience whatever is coming up for you. Journal as much as you wish. Before you move on, take a deep breath and relax. Take a moment to care for yourself.

## THE LANDSCAPE

As we entered the guided meditation, we immediately found ourselves in a place of moisture. There were cool vapors of water. Noticing that the refreshing, moist air was collecting on the skin just as it was collecting on the moss allowed us to understand that we were not the only thing sensing the water of this place. Water has a direct correlation to the emotional body, and the emotional pull of this place was welcoming. We entered a landscape that was very different than the dryness of the desert that we explored in the previous chapter.

The owl appeared on the old conifer tree—the tree of the ancestors and generations of growth and knowledge. It was suggested that the owl was watching over us and our ancestors' stories from the beginning and knows all that was seen and unseen, all that was spoken and unspoken, all that happened even during times of dissociation. The owl held the whole truth of all that is and was—even stories that were blocked out or hidden.

The shaman we sought was the owl. In our search, we were not able to depend upon our vision to guide us and encountered dissociation, disillusionment, and a sense of disembodiment. This was to help us return to times when this sensation may have felt a little familiar. Even if no actual memories came up, muscle memory drew us there in order to complete the trauma cycle.

We needed to feel through that place within our intuition. As the owl asked us to release our ego and our old emotions around life, it did so in order for us to seek more clearly, to see a bigger picture. The owl said, "Now, in the absence of light, you seek with clear vision." This suggested that intuition will be a better guide than the ego and old emotions.

## TIME OF DAY AND SEASON OF UNDERSTANDING

The time of day that corresponds with the owl is evening. It also corresponds with autumn—the season of change. During the twilight of the evening, and during the twilight of the year, it is more difficult to see with the naked eye. Things may disappear and reappear; pupils may expand or constrict as the light shifts. Things become dimmer and almost distorted in this space and time. This is a good thing, as it urges us to work with our other senses as we move about. Movement along the path that we are walking becomes more deliberate, our ears are tuned in to our surroundings to detect any unfamiliar sounds, and our sense of intuition is more alert. Hence, twilight is a wonderful time to learn how to develop all of our senses and to trust them during darker periods of life.

Additionally, autumn is a time of transition within the natural world. Mother Earth rolls though the cycle of life, death, and rebirth every year—it is natural. Autumn is a time of letting go, releasing, and, in a sense, dying. This is a great time for the emerging and merging of shadow work.

## MEDICINE WHEEL: DIRECTION AND ELEMENT

Now it is time to continue creating and working with the shadow medicine wheel. Remember that the medicine wheel is divided into four parts; this is the third part of four.

We continue on in a sunwise (clockwise) direction to the third portion of the circle. With the wisdom of the owl, we work in the west. We are working with the evening and autumn here, as these are times of change. When it is twilight, it is difficult to see what is in the light, and we begin to see what is in the shadows. We need to move through this time with other senses, as our eyesight could fool us.

Owl
West
Evening
Autumn
Water Element
Emotional Body
Understanding

Raven
East
Morning
Spring
Air Element
Mental Body
New Beginnings

Snake
South
Noontime
Summer
Fire Element
Spiritual Body
Acknowledgment

Working with the owl in the west

Here are recommendations for things to include in this section of your shadow medicine wheel:

- Write the word *west*.
- The animal that we are working with is the owl. Add this word as well, or draw or paste a picture of an owl within this section.
- Add your impressions of the waterfall and the landscape.
- Since we are working with twilight energy and the energy of the autumn, include these words or something else that represents these energies to you.
- The element that aligns with the west is water. Add the word *water* or any other representation of water that your creative side would like to include.
- Feel free to include your authentic touches in this section.

The element that aligns with the west is the element of water, and water aligns with the emotional realm. Within the emotional realm are the concepts of release and cleansing—this is why we found ourselves in a watery landscape in this chapter's Ingress and Portal meditation. In many ceremonial practices, water represents a baptism, a cleansing, a dedication, and a holy sanctifier. Water assists us in cleansing and releasing not only physically, but mentally, emotionally, and spiritually as well. As shamans, we must remember that the human body is about 70 percent water.

As you are becoming a shadow worker, it makes sense to continue the journey here, in the west, with the element of water and the emotional realm. This is a sacred space and time to release the ego and old emotions. Let go of the light and feel into the nighttime—the shadow. Now, you can begin to understand the shadow. You can see it from a bird's-eye view.

## A TOOL

Under the owl, we work with crystals. Crystals are close to my heart. Carrying a crystal connects me to the natural world and allows me to carry specific energy from Mother Earth. The way that these stones form teaches us a valuable lesson: when something is under great pressure for an extended amount of time, crystals can actualize. It was the same for me: it was under great pressure that my shadow formed, that my gifts formed, that I formed. It is with great pleasure that I share this information with you.

There are so many wonderful ways to connect and work with crystals. Whether you are a beginner or an expert, the energies of crystals will work with you on an individual level. One of the beautiful parts of working with crystals is being able to peer through them at various angles. Each angle refracts the light in a different way. This is symbolic of how to examine the shadow. If we look at it from many angles, we avoid getting stuck in a two-dimensional perspective. Moreover, we recognize that there are many points of view that we can examine the shadow from in order to gain understanding.

Crystals have mystical properties, including healing properties, protection aspects, manifestation attributes, and transformational properties. They can even be worked with as divination tools. They come in a myriad of shapes and forms, as well as a rainbow of colors. I invite you to explore working with crystals beyond shadow work, as they complement and enhance any spiritual practice.

## Acquiring Crystals

Crystals can be collected in a variety of ways. Sometimes a special stone or crystal is found while taking a walk in nature. If you take something from the natural world, I recommend leaving an offering of some sort as a way of respecting the land with the gift of equally exchanged energy.

Crystals can also be purchased from local metaphysical shops or online. Some are available for purchase in their uncut (not tumbled) state. If you prefer, you can purchase cut or tumbled stones. Cut stones are often made to be a specific shape, and tumbled stones have smoothed edges. Experiment with each type of crystals to see if you have a preference.

Maybe a crystal will be gifted to you. These are so special! I remember gifting a moonstone to my aunt Alice, a Navajo High Priestess of the Peyote Way. She received it, looked at it, held it up to the sky, and said, "You have traveled a long way to be in my hand." This is the sacredness of a stone. If you are still looking for a crystal to work with, you can always pray and ask a crystal to come to you. It will travel from any distance to be in your hand.

## How to Work with Crystals

Carrying crystals with you will enhance your energetic field, whether they are in your pocket or a piece of jewelry. Each crystal aligns with certain energetic vibrations. Different energies vibrate at certain frequencies and increase healing, cleansing, protective qualities, and more—the list is endless. I certainly recommend purchasing a book or taking a class to learn more about crystals, as each one carries different energies. There are so many ways to work with the energies of crystals that it would be impossible to cover them all here, so I encourage you to do more research.

I have some crystals placed around my house that boost the energies of clearing and protecting. For example, I have selenite in my windowsills to cleanse the energy in my home. I have onyx in my car to increase the energy of protection. I even have rose quartz under my bed to promote unconditional love while I am sleeping. If you decide to work with crystals by placing them around your dwelling, I highly recommend holding the crystal and asking it where it wants to be kept. Then, walk around your dwelling until you find the perfect place.

Another way to work with crystals is via a practice called *gridding*, also known as making a crystal grid. The art of gridding your home or workspace is relatively basic but extremely powerful. Crystals are placed in certain areas within a space; maybe there is one in each corner, or in each cardinal direction. When the crystals are placed, it is done with intention. Knowing the energy that a crystal represents allows it to be placed in the right location. It is important to note that the crystals used in a grid are up to you. Choose them with intention and playfulness. (I say "playfulness" because I have found that some of my most intuitive moments happened when I released my ego and played like a child.) Personally, I gridded my property with crystals. I simply walked the property line and dug a shallow hole in the east, south, west, and north, placing a crystal in each. I did this to secure my dwelling with a dynamic energetic field.

Another way to work with the energy of crystals is to adorn yourself with jewelry. Placing a crystal on the body is one way to hone their pure energy. For example, wearing a necklace that lands on one of the chakras will elevate that chakra in dynamic ways. I have tried this myself. There was a time when I was very shy. Public speaking was not my friend. I needed to open up my throat chakra, as I was beginning to understand that public speaking was in my future. I bought a blue crystal (blue agate) and wore it around my neck like a choker. I slowly began to speak my truth purely and calmly. Now, I love public speaking—my throat chakra is healthy.

## Working with the Chakras

In the Ingress and Portal section of this chapter, there was a quick reference to the rainbow that was cast by the waterfall. This is a perfect segue for talking about the rainbow and its correlation to the chakra system. The colors of the rainbow align with the basic seven-chakra model. As I shared in chapter 3, chakras are vital energy centers of life force. To amplify a certain energy, choose a crystal that aligns with the color of the corresponding chakra.

Aligning crystals with the colors of the chakra system provides so much insight. Here are some general takeaways:

- Dark crystals align with protection and grounding.
- Red crystals align with the root chakra ("I have the right to be").
- Orange crystals align with the sacral chakra ("I have the right to connect").
- Yellow crystals align with the solar plexus chakra ("I own my will; I am").
- Green crystals align with the heart chakra ("I have the right to love and be loved").

- Blue crystals align with the throat chakra ("I have the right to share and express; I have a voice").

- Indigo and purple crystals align with the third eye chakra ("I have the right to see and perceive").

- Purple and white crystals align with the crown chakra ("I am one with everything").

This is a very basic approach to working with crystals, but it is a system that serves us well. In the following pages, I have provided meanings and mystical properties of specific crystals as a basic, easy-to-understand resource.

## Black, Silver, and Gray Crystals

A common theme of black, silver, and gray crystals is that they are protective, as they entrap negative energy. They also help detoxify energy and promote groundedness. Here are some specific black, silver, or gray crystals and their correspondences.

- **Tourmaline:** Tourmaline is a good stone to carry with you when you feel like you need an extra level of protection. It removes energetic blockages and balances personal energy as well as the energy within a space. Tourmaline can also help with dyslexia and hand-eye coordination.

- **Jet:** This crystal can help with mood swings, depression, migraines, and epilepsy. Jet is known to be a very personal stone and carries the energy of the owner, so it isn't a good one to pass around.

- **Obsidian:** This is another protective stone that gives the holder strength. It also helps with the digestion of anything that is hard to accept, physically, emotionally, mentally, and spiritually. Also, obsidian helps with circulation in the physical body.

- **Apache Tear:** This stone helps with forgiveness and alleviates sadness. This is a good stone to carry when dealing with depression or while mourning the loss of someone or something. It also helps with muscle spasms.

- **Onyx:** This crystal assists with making wise decisions and is centering. It also balances yin and yang energies.

## Brown Crystals

Common themes of brown crystals include connecting with the earth, grounding, and cleansing or purifying energy. These stones can be protective as well as stabilizing and centering. Here are some brown crystals and their correspondences.

- **Smoky Quartz:** This crystal helps to increase concentration. It can also alleviate nightmares, depression, headaches, and stress.

- **Bronzite:** Bronzite promotes a sense of harmony within yourself and within any situation. It increases self-assertion and willfulness. This crystal also helps with chronic exhaustion.

- **Desert Rose:** This crystal helps with connective tissue, bone health, and osteoporosis. It also provides an individual with sound judgment and insight.

- **Brown Jasper:** Brown jasper increases night vision and strengthens the immune system. It can clear pollutants and toxins and cleanses organs and skin.

- **Tiger's Eye:** This crystal assists with sight and healing of the eyes. It integrates the brain's right and left hemispheres, the creative and logical aspects of self. It provides emotional balance and better perception.

## Red Crystals

Red crystals resonate with the root chakra. Broadly, they assist with bodily concerns that have to do with the blood, such as hemorrhages and inflammation. Here are some red crystals and their correspondences.

- **Garnet:** This stone can attract love. It helps with blood diseases and regenerates the body (heart, lungs, cells, etc.). Garnet also assists with the assimilation of minerals and vitamins in the body.

- **Ruby:** Ruby increases the energies of leadership and courage. This crystal heightens awareness and concentration. It can also enhance immunity and vitality.

- **Jasper:** This crystal decreases electromagnetic and environmental pollution, radiation, and stress. It helps to balance the mineral content of the body. Jasper is a great shaman stone, as it connects us with the earth.

## Orange Crystals

Orange crystals correspond with the sacral chakra. They boost creativity and also supply grounded energy to get a project finished. Here are some orange crystals and their correspondences.

- **Carnelian:** This stone increases an individual's analytic ability and concentration. It also boosts courage, improves a weak memory, and helps with anger issues. It can assist with metabolism, food assimilation, and kidney function.

- **Sunstone:** Sunstone increases self-worth and self-empowerment. It also helps with SAD (Seasonal Affective Disorder) as it brings happiness and purifies the energetic field, just like the sun.

- **Fire Agate:** This crystal assists with getting you going and boosts motivation. It helps release fears, lessens insecurity, and can mitigate addictive behaviors. It also helps with hot flashes.

## Yellow and Gold Crystals

Yellow crystals resonate with the solar plexus chakra and intellect, the mind, and balancing emotions. Gold crystals have long been associated with masculine energy (whereas silver is feminine energy). Additionally, these stones invite in wealth and abundance. Gold is conductive, so any crystal can be placed on a gold chain and worn as a necklace to allow the energy of the crystal to connect with the individual's energy more quickly. Here are some yellow or gold crystals and their correspondences.

- **Citrine:** This crystal decreases our sensitivity to environmental influences, such as a bad or toxic environment. It increases feelings of optimism and helps us let go of the past. Citrine can also increase an individual's concentration levels. It promotes clarity and individuality.

- **Amber:** Amber improves memory and helps with decision-making. It promotes wisdom and peace.

- **Yellow Sapphire:** This stone has a great supportive energy that can help us achieve any ambition. It soothes overactive body systems (such as the stomach, gallbladder, liver, and spleen) and promotes peace of mind.

- **Beryl:** Beryl increases courage and reduces stress. One can also obtain blue beryl, which will help with clear communication.

## Green Crystals

Green crystals resonate with the heart chakra. They aid in emotional healing and encourage a healthy heart. The color green represents life force and growth, as seen in nature. This makes green stones a great option for prosperity and wealth. Here are some specific green crystals and their correspondences.

- **Malachite:** Malachite assists with transformation. It helps to release past-life trauma, childhood trauma, and stress and protects against the evil eye.

- **Green Agate:** This stone increases self-confidence and concentration. It also helps resolve disputes because it enhances mental and emotional flexibility.

- **Green Fluorite:** This crystal improves the connection to higher energy and can offer stability while moving through an ascension process. It is a good stone to carry to calm feelings of worry. Green fluorite also assists with coordination, self-confidence, and centering.

- **Bloodstone:** Bloodstone helps with circulation and healthy blood flow and can even purify the blood. Because of this quality, it is a great stone to keep nearby post-surgery. It also revitalizes love and other emotions of the heart.

- **Seraphinite:** This is known as the angel stone. Seraphinite increases enlightenment and spiritual vibrations. It can help with weight loss and reduces muscle tension in the neck.

- **Jade:** Jade is a stone of vitality and longevity. It promotes self-sufficiency. This crystal is also known for protecting children.

- **Turquoise:** This crystal is known to promote healing of all types: physical, emotional, mental, and spiritual. It is said to bridge heaven and earth. To some, this is the ultimate "heal all" stone.

## Blue Crystals

The color blue aligns with the throat chakra and encourages us to speak our truth with compassion. Blue stones encourage self-expression and reflect the sky and the heavens, lifting us up. Here are some blue crystals and their correspondences.

- **Azurite:** This stone can promote healing after a crisis. It brings truth and justice to any situation. Azurite also helps with mental processing.

- **Blue Calcite:** Blue calcite helps us recuperate and reduces pain on all levels: physical, emotional, mental, and spiritual. This stone increases motivation and promotes healing and purification within the body. Blue calcite also balances the energies of giving and receiving in any relationship or situation.

- **Angelite:** This crystal increases awareness. It promotes compassion and connects us with the gentleness of spirit. Angelite also assists with rebirth and transformation.

- **Celestite:** Celestite assists with creativity and all art forms. It promotes peaceful coexistence and increases mental clarity. This is a high-vibrational stone that promotes existential awareness.

- **Lapis Lazuli:** This stone helps us seek clarity in any situation. It is a high-vibrational stone that has been used for thousands of years.

## Indigo and Purple Crystals

Indigo and purple crystals align with the third eye chakra. Generally, these crystals create spirituality on the earthly plane. They also align us with higher states of consciousness. Here are some specific indigo or purple crystals and their correspondences.

- **Amethyst:** This stone promotes our connection to the Divine by providing multidimensional awareness. It is worn by many individuals to boost their spiritual awareness.

- **Charoite:** This stone teaches us to accept the present moment as perfect.

## White and Clear Crystals

White and clear crystals align with the crown chakra and have many wonderful aspects. Here are some specific white or clear crystals and their correspondences.

- **Selenite:** Selenite is known to be an all-purpose cleansing stone, as it cleanses the energy of any space that it is in. If you need to cleanse any object (jewelry, tarot cards, another stone, etc.), you can place the object on or by a piece of selenite.

- **Diamond:** This crystal is formed under a lot of pressure and is at the top of the Mohs Hardness Scale. Hence, when we carry a diamond, we carry its strength. Diamonds lend us the fortitude to withstand challenging situations.

- **Clear Quartz:** This stone records the energy and vibration that it is charged with. For example, I can hold clear quartz during meditation with the intention of recording the energy of that meditation. After the meditation is finished, I can seal its energy into the clear quartz by asking the stone to hold that energy within. Then, when I carry that clear quartz, I am also carrying the energy of my meditation with me.

## SUMMARY

This is stage three of our four-stage process of shadow work. In this chapter, we worked toward understanding the wisdom of the shadow. We worked with the spirit of the owl, which has the ability to see beyond the naked eye. The owl encouraged us to perceive with all five senses as well as instinct and intuition. Other connections included the time of day (the evening time, as the sun is going down and shadows are beginning to dominate) and the landscape (a waterfall and the skeleton of an old tree, representing our emotions and ancestors). We worked with crystals, which can align with the chakras and bring us special messages from the owl, ancestors, the shadow, and our spirit. Knowing more of this natural world and its natural elements, you are now able to listen. Breathe in this place, and return if and when you feel the call. You carry this chapter's wisdom within you now!

# 8

# ACCEPTING THE SHADOW (THE WOLF)

This is the fourth and final chapter in the shadow work journey. In this chapter, we will seek integration and knowledge to respect the entire journey of the shadow. This has been quite the adventure so far, and I am hoping at this point you have gained and grown from this shadow work. Now, we will achieve even more greatness and have more respect for ourselves and what we have been through.

Together, we move into this chapter with the sole intention of gaining knowledge and respect that we might not have had otherwise: knowledge and respect for the fact that we all have a shadow side; knowledge and respect for where our shadows came from; knowledge and respect for a deeper understanding of the shadow side. Remember, as we approach the final shaman and this final connection with the shadow, we must release judgment. We must approach the shadow with curiosity and an open heart and mind. In many societies, cultures, and communities, we are pressured to ignore the shadow and its existence within our consciousness and in our lives. As mentioned earlier, the shadow does not disappear if we ignore it; it still exists, and it will come out sideways if not embraced. In fact, the shadow holds a knowledge that we haven't been able to fully understand until now. Now, we are able to gain knowledge and respect with the guidance of the wolf.

In this chapter, we will work with the spirit of the wolf— another animal that is as taboo as the shadow in certain communities. Although the wolf has been villainized in legends and lore, there is a mysticism around wolves that may not be fully understood. A wolf pack is able to live together, hunt together, and raise their young together. Unity, togetherness, and loyalty are key aspects that the wolves teach us. All of us are alone at times; wouldn't it be nice to be a part of the pack? The truth is that the shadow side knows about unity, togetherness, and loyalty too. Hence, as we embrace the shadow, we embrace more of ourselves.

## WOLF ANIMAL TOTEM

In this section, we will cover a variety of aspects of the wolf to connect to its energy. The first way to do this is to recognize basic attributes based on its characteristics and how the wolf moves within the world. We will also understand the animal totem by observing some personality traits of the wolf. Feel free to add any personal experiences or insights that you have to this description.

When the wolf is our teacher, it brings us wisdom about how to be in the world: how to move, how to explore, how to connect with a pack. Wolves are very social beings, and they teach us how to be social beings by showing respect to each other. Some storytellers speculate that the wolf showed mankind how to smile. When a wolf shows us its teeth, we immediately gain respect for it. This is like the universal language that we show each other as humans: we smile. When someone smiles at me, I recognize that they are addressing me directly—they are aware of me. A quick, respectful exchange occurs.

With its tough hide and thick fur, the wolf is prepared for colder environments and will not shy away from any given situation. The wolf has all four paws on the ground. Hence, it is very connected to Mother Earth. Earth is the element of the physical realm and manifestation. The wolf totem is a teacher, showing us how to respect ourselves and the world around us.

Wolves are great hunters; they can take down animals that are much larger than themselves. Wolves hunt within a pack, an organized approach of many different positions, perspectives, and possibilities working together. They bay at the moon and call out to each other to find their way back home. When we are feeling lost or we don't know which way to go, we can call upon the spirit of the wolf—it will lead us back to the heartbeat of Mother Earth.

The wolf feels the pull of the moon. The moon can be seen as the reflection of light within the darkness of night. Does the moon call the wolf, or does the wolf call the moon? A mystical dance takes place between the spirit of the moon and the spirit of the wolf. Additionally, the wolf makes its own path in the woods—it doesn't follow the most traveled path. In such, it is very aware and able to discern the environment and which direction it would like to go. Hence, the spirit of the wolf will take us through this final adventure as we seek knowledge and respect for the shadow.

The wolf is taboo to many traditional Navajo people, including my father. Hence, I will share a story from outside the Navajo Way out of respect for my tribal elders. In Norse lore, Fenrir the Wolf was known to be a child of a giantess and the trickster god Loki, also taboo in many communities. Fenrir kept growing and growing, and he became much larger than any ordinary wolf. He was feared because of his size, so the gods restrained him. In the process, Fenrir bit off the hand of the god Tyr, who was the god of justice.

With this legend in mind—and considering all the similar stories of the "big bad wolf"—it is safe to say that the wolf is seen as a very taboo animal. However, many of us interact with descendants of the wolf on a regular basis! The wolf is just one animal that humans have domesticated over the years. In fact, the dog is a domesticated descendant of the wolf. Wolves have so much to teach us.

## KNOWLEDGE LEADS TO RESPECT

Here, I share a familiar refrain: All is energy! Energy seeks its freedom. Energy wants to be known and respected for what it is. When we do not respect energy for what it is, it is left dishonored or even denied, and that can cause problems. When we imprison the shadow, it suffers, and we suffer. Because the shadow doesn't disappear—it simply changes forms until it is acknowledged and respected. When the shadow is looking for respect, it can morph into something stronger in order to gain our attention and respect. If the shadow is embraced, it will teach us the wonders of the world beyond our wildest imagination.

In order to be able to embrace the shadow, we need to sit quietly, with focus. The ability to know thyself and respect thyself is earned. Here comes the totem of the wolf—the teacher with all four feet on the ground. If you are still experiencing the reactive side rather than the proactive side, now is the time to sense safety within the pack of wolves! You must be safe to feel all of your feelings; you must be safe to experience everything that you have gone through. Do not be threatened when you finally get to feel; this pack of wolves will accept you and your shadow.

With a deep inhale, the wolf can pick up a scent in the air. With a tilt of its head, it can pick up a sound in the wind. And under the light of the moon, it will call for you and your shadow to come forth—to come home.

## INGRESS AND PORTAL

I invite you to settle into an environment that is comfortable for you, one where you will not be disturbed so that the beautiful silhouette of your shadow feels safe enough to come forth. Light a candle or make a cup of tea if that helps you relax. Set your journal nearby so you are able to access it after completing your journey.

This is the organic part of working with the shadow. This is the time when we allow the shadow to speak to us individually and authentically. Working with the shadow is sacred work; you will be directed and guided by your truth and the truth of your personal shadow. The shadow's truth may be a truth that you haven't seen very clearly until now.

First, set sacred space for this working. Feel free to read this part aloud if you wish:

> I am creating a sacred space and a sacred time. I draw a circle around this space and time and declare it sacred. It is within this space that I am whole; I am loved; I am me. There is a reason that I have found myself here. I am ready to meet my shadow, and I know that my shadow has led me here and is ready to meet me too. Being here confirms that I have made an agreement to meet my shadow in this holy, sacred space. I welcome the Divine as it has revealed itself to me to walk with me here. I welcome the spirit of the wolf and its knowledge to accompany me here. I welcome my shadow with great honor and respect. Be here with me now. And so it is!

With this statement, you allow the ego and assumptions to slowly drift away. You have created a safe space committed to curiosity and discovery. You are now in a sacred space and a sacred time.

Begin your breathwork. Inhale through the nose. Hold your breath, then exhale through the mouth. Continue to breathe in this manner for at least a minute or two. This moves you from a conscious state into a more relaxed, observant position.

> *Breathe in this place. Sizzling charcoal and evergreen resin scent the cold forest air that you inhale through your nostrils. Your breath clouds only briefly, lost to*

*the warmth of the small fire that burns before you.
The snap of twigs as they are engulfed by flames
punctuates the silence of the great aspen forest that
surrounds you on all sides as far as the eye can see.
Near you, the fire's glow reflects off the snow's icy face.
The fire's reflection shifts and dances on paper-white
trunks, giving the illusion of movement within the
stillness of the tall trees protruding through the snow.
Gazing up high on one of the trunks, you see the
healed scars of bear claws that once slashed through
bark, marking their territory for all to see. It is here
that you seek the shaman of this place.*

*The small fire before you flares yellow, then falters
in flame, having rapidly consumed its fuel. Shadows
shift direction as the blue light of a full moon now casts
shadows from above, illuminating the thin smoke of
red embers dimming before you.*

*"If you were god, what question would you
ask yourself?" speaks the forest as you gaze into
its moonlit stillness. Blurred tree trunks gleam like
cathedral columns beneath their canopy of branches.
Far away, you see movement between the trunks and
hear the crunch of four-legged footfalls breaking the
crust as a form makes its way in your direction. You
sense no menace as the she wolf nears you; she has
not come for you. She seeks, but it is not you that is
sought. Head low and tail down, she stops opposite
the cooling embers. Momentarily, she sniffs the snow,
then raises her snout to taste the cold night air as she
circles in a counterclockwise direction before you,*

*beginning to whimper apprehensively and summoning up yipes of concern.*

*The yipes and whimpers are louder now, and pained. She sits, raises her head, and begins to bay toward the treetops. Her song calls out to the ones who are late returning to the den. The she wolf is the call of return for those who wander in the shadows—hers is the voice they gather to and around, both the young and the old. It is a voice in the wind that speaks of counsel long forgotten.*

*Under the rays of moonlight, wolves appear like ghosts from between the trunks. All the wolves gather behind her on the frost-white snow within the shadows. They all peer at you in silence, as does she. Their numbers take you aback as you wonder how you could not have seen at least a glimpse of their presence before.*

*It is said that to offer attention to the forest is to immerse with its spirit, and in return, its spirit will immerse with you. The forest is home to the wolf, man's first teacher. When a wolf is born, it is connected to all. Through this process, you are no longer observing or being observed; you have become one with the pack. The pack has become one with you, and through them, you are connected to the trees and the moon—oneness within the greatness of all.*

*Understanding more of the nature of the wolf and the forest, you are now able to listen…*

*Breathe in this place and return when needed.*
*You carry the breadth of the wolf and the landscape*
*within you now.*

Slowly move out of your meditative state and return to the space that you are in. Gently wiggle your fingers and toes as you return to your surroundings. Allow your state of consciousness to be present with your body.

## Journal Prompts

I invite you to reread the previous section while still in a relaxed state. With your journal next to you, reread each word. As you read, reference this section for complementary journal prompts, taking a moment to pause and journal about what you are experiencing.

As you "breathe in this place":

1. How does your physical body feel about this place?

2. Are there any emotions that are coming up for you?

3. Which thoughts cross your mind?

4. What are you sensing with your five senses? Describe any smells, any sounds that you hear, any sensations you feel as you touch the grass, etc.

5. Are you seeing or becoming aware of anything else within this landscape? If so, write it down.

As you experience the fire, the forest, and the full moon:

6. What are you experiencing, if anything, when you are sitting before the fire? What sensations or thoughts does it bring to mind?

7. As you observe the fire's glow on the aspen trees, how does this experience speak to you?

8. Write down whatever sensations, thoughts, or experiences you are having under the full moon.

9. The night is very still. Write down how being here makes you feel or any sensations that you are experiencing in this stillness.

10. The forest asks, "If you were god, what question would you ask yourself?" Contemplate on this and write down your thoughts and feelings.

During the first encounter with the she wolf:

11. As the she wolf begins to approach the fire and you catch a glimpse of her, how does this make you feel?

12. As you watch the she wolf baying out and calling for her pack and all of them show up, what does this make you think of, if anything? Do you feel something? Please write down any thoughts or feelings.

13. As you observe the other wolves appearing, does this strike up any thoughts or feelings within you?

After the other wolves appear:

14. As the wolf pack begins to connect with each other, does this bring up any thoughts or feelings?

15. As you begin to connect with the wolf pack, how are you experiencing this? Does it cause you to think of anything, or does it bring up any emotions? Please write down your experience.

Now, take a few moments to simply feel and experience whatever is coming up for you. Journal as much as you wish. The rest of this chapter will assist you in understanding your experience. Before you move on, take a deep breath and relax. Take a moment to care for yourself.

## THE LANDSCAPE

In the Ingress and Portal section, we got a quick glimpse of aspen trees. Aspen trees are one of the largest, if not the largest, organisms on the face of the earth. This is because aspen trees will connect their root systems to communicate with other aspen trees—when their root systems connect, they become one larger organism. A grove of aspen trees typically shares a singular root system.

We also read this statement: "Gazing up high on one of the trunks, you see the healed scars of bear claws that once slashed through bark, marking their territory for all to see." This sentence helped us understand that we were in a forest with other wild animals. Moreover, the bear shows us that there are times to hibernate and rest: Once we emerge from hibernation, we have a deeper understanding and knowledge of who we are and how we would like to move forward.

The forest was the home of the wolf pack. The pack reminded us that there are generational truths, and generational shadows may appear or reveal themselves to us. Not all shadows come from this lifetime; some are carried over from generation to generation. As the wolves approached us with the spirit of a pack or family, we remembered this truth.

Please take a moment to reflect on the shadow journey once again. What was the shadow beginning to show you? You may have run into generational shadows—simply be aware.

## TIME OF DAY AND SEASON OF RESPECT

In this book, the wolf shows up during the nighttime. Its season then becomes the winter, a time to go within and to be silent, to rest and assimilate. In the winter, under the full moon, we gather with our pack to connect and immerse in something greater than the light side: We are being called to merge the light side with the shadow side. The wild wolf pack is not afraid of the light side; the wild wolf pack is not afraid of the shadow. The wolf pack fully accepts us and teaches us to be unafraid of the wildness within.

In the dead of winter, in the stillness of the cold, the shadow is fully present and cannot be ignored. It is a human belief that we should only be light, without shadow—the natural world does not hold this concept. It is a human belief that we cannot fully be who and what we are naturally made to be. Remember, no matter how much sun there is, there is an equal balance of night and shadow. If we ignore this aspect of ourselves, we are ignoring who we are fully. When the wolf pack looks at us, they see us fully. They will only accept us fully if we are able to accept ourselves fully—both the light and the shadow. Take a deep breath and decide. Here are the final tasks: Will you accept yourself? Can you respect yourself?

One night as I was writing this book, I had a dream. I dreamed that my shadow appeared to me and gave me a hug. She looked exactly like me, yet she carried the scars of my pain. She told me she was there throughout all the times in my life that I felt alone. She told me that she is the one who understands my reality, my perspectives, and how I came to be. At that moment, I returned the hug, as I felt seen and understood.

I held my shadow and told her "Thank you." She relaxed, and we began to merge together. I then saw the words *WE'RE ALL ONE*. I began to understand: I was never alone. Then my shadow dropped the second L and moved the words together. I now read *WE'RE ALONE*. My shadow had showed me that when I felt alone, she was with me. And being alone was not what I thought it was—my shadow was always there.

My shadow is my ally. She is the one I need to connect with, to know, because she knows and respects me for who and what I am. Now, I don't have to look for external approval or under-standing (if I receive it, that is a bonus), for my shadow knows me and accepts me, and I know and respect my shadow. We're All One—We're AlOne, in the best way possible.

## MEDICINE WHEEL: DIRECTION AND ELEMENT

Now it is time to complete the shadow medicine wheel. This is the fourth and final part of the shadow medicine wheel.

We continue on in a sunwise (clockwise) direction to the final quadrant of the circle. With the wisdom of the wolf, we work with the north. We are working with the energy of the nighttime and the wintertime here, times of acceptance and finality. During the night, we reflect on what the morning, noon, and evening brought to us. This is a time to accept what we experienced and the knowledge it revealed to us; we respect it for what it is.

In this section, we will complete the medicine wheel, but more importantly, we need to take a moment to reflect on all that we have moved through: the recognition of the shadow in the east; the acknowledgment of the shadow in the south; the understanding of the shadow in the west; and, finally, the knowledge of the shadow that leads to respect for the shadow—and respect for ourselves.

Working with the wolf in the north

In the north, in the winter, in the dead of night, we sat in front of a fire with a pack of wolves. There was no light beyond the fire and the glow of the full moon. It was here that we were able to put all of the pieces together and begin to respect the shadow side.

From a shamanic point of view, the north holds the element of earth. It is the place where all is actualized; all has manifested. In the north, we are finally able to see the full circle—we have completed the cycle.

Here are recommendations for things to include in this fourth and final quadrant of your shadow medicine wheel:

- Write the word *north*.

- The animal that we are working with is the wolf. Add this word as well, or draw or paste a picture of a wolf or wolf pack within this section.

- Add any language around your impressions of the forest or woodlands.

- Since we are working with nighttime energy and the energy of the winter, include these words or something else that represents these energies to you. I include a starry night sky or snowflakes falling all around.

- The element that aligns with the north is earth. Add the word *earth* or any other representation of earth that your creative side would like to include.

- Feel free to include your authentic touches in this section.

The element of earth aligns with the physical realm, the realm of manifestation. The concept of manifestation allows us to recognize that every experience has led to this moment. Everything—including every thought, feeling, and action that we have experienced—has created what is manifesting here. Whether or not the light side remembered and processed everything, some thoughts, feelings, and actions may still lie dormant within us—

but the shadow remembers and knows what the light side may want to forget, and it is here to assist with a complete integration. This is the moment when we are able to see a reflection of our complete self, our full self. What we asked to come forward will now do so in the physical realm.

This is why we found ourselves under a full moon in front of a fire. This was not only a time of reflection and revelation, it was also a time when we were quiet enough to understand everything that had happened, everything that led us to this point. If you were able to see and to embrace the larger picture, this was the time to respect your shadow and the wisdom that it holds for you. It has held this wisdom, wanting to share it with you, but waiting until you were in a place where you were safe enough to accept it.

As we are becoming shadow workers, it makes sense to complete the journey here, in the north, with the elements of earth and the physical realm. The physical realm is where everything manifests, including the light and the shadow, the accepted and the rejected parts of ourselves. It is the realm of true existence.

If you have not yet done so, this is a sacred space and time to release the ego. Release the old ideas or personification of self and decide to have respect for the current version of yourself. Sit in the aspen grove, in the silence of the full moon, with the wolves staring back at you. Can you relax and be yourself? Here, you are accepted and respected, but only if you accept and respect yourself. This is the final frontier. The shaman is within you—acceptance and respect are up to you.

# A TOOL

The moon is the main tool of the spirit of the wolf, though there is a second tool we can utilize when working with the wolf. The second tool is a little more obscure: it is the tool of connecting with others. In this section, I will refer to this as *togetherness*. The act of togetherness is revealed in the pack of wolves. Working together and connecting can be one of the greatest tools; it intensifies a working. Of course, there are practices that can only be done in solitude. However, this is the final chapter of becoming a shadow worker, and it is time to pursue togetherness with the shadow self. The moon and the act of togetherness can be a pact with you and your shadow. Remember the message from my dream: *We're All One; We're AlOne*.

The moon is an illuminated body within the night sky. Due to its shadow, and the shadow the earth casts upon it, it grows from a new moon into a full moon in about two weeks, moving back from a full moon to a new moon over the following two weeks. The moon continues this cycle every twenty-eight to thirty days, so it repeats thirteen times a year. Sometimes, we experience a blue moon. A blue moon occurs when two full moons appear within one Gregorian calendar month.

The moon has a gravitational pull with the earth. This gravitational pull affects the tides of Earth's oceans, creating high tide and low tide around the globe. This natural effect of the moon's gravitational pull on the water that covers the majority of the earth can be directly translated to the gravitational pull the moon has on us, as the human body is about 70 percent water. If you have ever worked the nightshift during a full moon, you have certainly noticed that stranger sides to people come out under a full moon. This confirms to me that the gravitational pull the moon has on the oceans is a macro understanding of the micro gravitational pull that the moon has on us individually. It heightens our self-expression.

Why do wolves bay at the moon? In my research, it appears that this idea might be more legend than actual truth. However, the artistic expression of a wolf howling at the moon is epic and speaks to the human soul. When a wolf is howling at the full moon, is the wolf calling to the moon or responding to it? I believe that both can simultaneously be true; I believe that it is a balanced relationship between the wolf and the moon. Additionally, I believe that this is the same balance we can have with our dreams. Since we are focused on the shadow in this book, I will ask the same question about us and the shadow side: are we calling to the shadow, or is the shadow calling to us? Again, I believe that both are simultaneously true. If you are reading this book, something called you to it. Hence, we are a part of this balanced relationship of howling at the moon, calling forth our dreams, and becoming a shadow worker. The moon, our dreams, and the shadow are calling us too. We bay at the moon, calling upon it as we would call our dreams to come forth, for within the moon are the hidden treasures the soul seeks. The wolf reveals an obvious truth: The moon that you gaze upon is the same moon that I gaze upon; the moon that you gaze upon is the same moon that those who came before you saw. The wisdom of the wolf teaches us that we are all connected and watched over by the light of the moon.

As a shamanic practitioner, I invite you to work with the cycle of the moon. One way to do this is to sit under the night sky for at least ten minutes. As you sit, work with the five basic senses (sight, sound, touch, smell, and taste) to record what you are experiencing. Do this each night from the new moon to the full moon. (You can begin at any point in the lunar cycle; simply record what phase the moon is in and what you experience.) You may find that as the moon changes, the sights and sounds of the natural world change with it. This is one way to personally connect with the phases of the moon and how they speak with you. If you already have a relationship with the moon, allow this exercise to intensify or deepen it.

I have developed a personal relationship with the moon and its light that includes charging or clearing magical items under the moonlight as well as moon bathing. Charging or clearing a magical item is as simple as placing the item in a safe place under the light of the full moon to allow the item to absorb the energy of the moon. Moon bathing is much like sunbathing, though it involves resting in the light of the moon rather than the sun and absorbing the energy that you feel. Some people place a covered dish or jar of water under the light of the moon to charge the water magically and will either drink the water or add it to a bath or magical spell. There are endless ways to connect to and work with the moon.

There are several other ways I harness the moon's energy. First, I connect with the moon in order to more deeply connect with the natural world, as the moon's light sees all of Earth. I draw my consciousness up to the moon and imagine that I am looking at the earth from the moon's position. This allows me to see the world from a completely different point of view. If I want to connect with a jungle, a mountain, or a desert, for example, I may imagine that I am standing on the moon and observing these landscapes from above. This exercise allows me to engage in different perspectives of the natural world and the earth. Because the moon is visible everywhere on the globe, when we connect with the moon, we have a direct connection to other areas of the world, expanding our worldview and our understanding of how we see the world.

I also work with the spirit of the moon when I am traveling. I do this for protection. The moon that I see outside my window at home is the same moon that I see when I am traveling. Hence, before I go on a trip, I look up at the moon and ask its energy to watch over me on my travels. This brings me comfort, and the moon becomes a common ally on my journey.

I work with the spirit of the moon to connect with loved ones who have passed on and my ancestors. For a moment, I focus my attention on the moon and allow my consciousness to explore the idea that the moon I am looking at is the same moon they looked at too. This brings a sense of oneness. I feel a sense of connectedness with the ancestors I have met as well as the ancestors I haven't met. In this sense, the moon becomes a focal point between me and everything and everyone else.

The spirit of the moon can connect us to the shadow side, for the light side and the shadow side both see the moon. The energy of the moon gives the light side and the shadow side a common ground for connection, unity, integration, and togetherness.

Let's take a quick detour here to investigate the concept of togetherness and what it can produce. It is not farfetched to believe that when we come together with a focus, we create a dynamic energy that far outweighs the sum of the individual energy. It is a bit like saying that one plus one equals three. When two individuals get together, they are able to create another individual—one plus one equals three. This is not only true in the physical realm; it is true in the mental realm as well. When we are in dialogue with others, we are engaging in a type of communication that promotes wholeness rather than division. Dialogue occurs when we decide how to reason or think together—and when this occurs, a common mind will arise.[17] Or shall I say a third mind? Dialogue creates shared meaning; it connects us to each other and to the natural world. It also connects us to ourselves, including the shadow side.

Think of a situation when there was a noticeable flow—a dialogue—between two or more individuals. Ideas began to collect and coalesce; everyone collaborated to such a degree that they were beginning to "think together." Each person still held individual thoughts, yet they blended together into what some call *groupthink*. Within this energetic dynamic, there is the sensation of minds being connected to such a degree that individuals can't always differentiate between themselves and each other. An individual may wonder, *I am not sure if I came up with that idea or if they did.* The truth is that they came up with the idea together—one plus one equals three. This is the magic of togetherness. There is the understanding that there is something beyond us at work here.

For artists, this is the moment of recognition that what is being created has a life of its own and is flowing through you. For musicians, this is the moment the song begins to sing itself. For writers, this is the moment your book becomes alive, and you almost feel as though it is writing itself through you. For magicians, this is the moment your magical working directs itself, and you are its conduit. This is the tool of togetherness. Togetherness is the magic that happens when you release yourself to what is occurring and allow it to flow through you.

17. Bohm, *On Dialogue*, xviii.

This synchronicity is also witnessed within the natural world. In fact, it is the sustaining element of the natural world. The natural world thinks and expresses together. Consider the symbiotic relationships that form within the natural world; the connections between plants, animals, and the land are amazing. Scientifically speaking, we can refer to symbiotic relationships as a biosphere. At times, a biosphere can become imbalanced, and some organisms may become extinct. Relationships, connections, and togetherness are as vital to the natural world as they are to humankind. Togetherness is one of our most powerful tools.

Let's explore the topic of togetherness within the natural world. Of course, togetherness is witnessed within a pack of wolves. But have you ever seen a field of horses? When one horse looks up for a moment, all the other horses look in the same direction. The synchronicity appears to be almost telepathic; it is as though there is an interconnection between the horses. This is groupthink. This is the power of the tool of togetherness.

A whole book could be written on the art of togetherness, so I will simply state that the most important aspects of togetherness are showing up with an open heart and an open mind. We also have to agree to think together. Thinking together doesn't mean that we will always see eye to eye; however, it requires the ability to respect another's perspective even if it is opposite of your own. Think about it this way: If a group of people sat in a circle and placed an object in the middle of the circle, they would each perceive different aspects of the object even though they were all looking at the same thing. Groupthink is respecting what the individual—who may be on the opposite side of the circle, so to speak—is witnessing, as it will create a more complete picture. If we only see things from our perspective, we miss out on the bigger picture. If we want to better understand, we need to approach life with the attitude of "I see and understand more when I listen to others." It takes a strong mind to entertain a concept that it does not adopt. Be flexible and consider concepts that others might present—you will learn more than you think.

Here is one last example of the power of togetherness and groupthink. I once heard a story about five blind individuals and an elephant. While these five individuals could not see the elephant, they were able to touch it for a few moments. After each of them touched the elephant, they gathered in a circle to discuss what an elephant is. The first individual described the elephant as a big leafy object. The second individual disagreed and stated that the elephant was a snakelike being. The third individual spoke up and said that they were both wrong; the elephant was like a rope with a bushy, hairy tail at the end. The fourth stated, "You are all wrong. The elephant is like a tree stump—strong and sturdy." Finally, the fifth individual stated, "You are all mistaken. The elephant is a massive globe of energy." They argued and argued, as each of them knew what they had felt and experienced.

The truth is that they were all correct; however, they were assuming that the elephant was only what they had individually experienced and nothing more than that. If the individuals had released the idea that what they experienced was the entire elephant, they would have had a different conversation. The first individual had felt the elephant's ear, which is why they described it as a big leafy object. The second experienced the elephant's trunk as a snakelike being. The third experienced the elephant's tail as a rope. The fourth experienced the elephant's leg as a tree stump. The fifth experienced the body of the elephant as a massive globe of energy. They each experienced a truth. Togetherness would have allowed these five individuals to join in groupthink and actually perceive the elephant in its entirety. With the power of dialogue, we agree to think together, even when we perceive different things.

## SUMMARY

This was stage four of our four-stage process of shadow work. In this chapter, we worked with the spirit of the wolf and the wolf pack. In this way, we learned how to immerse ourselves in the shadow and how to respect the shadow. Other connections included the nighttime, which can be frightening as we cannot see very well. It is the same when we are working with the shadow: it can be dark and frightening, but it is part of the process. Additionally, we found ourselves in a forest of aspen trees. The aspen trees were all connected through the root system, and it is the same with humanity: even when we stand alone, we are not alone. The wolf pack shares this same message.

I am proud to say we have completed the full cycle of the shadow work journey. If you are reading this, I am so proud of you. We are not shamans because the road is easy—we are shamans because we have moved through many levels of this multidimensional experience with our balance still intact.

Namaste. The shaman in me recognizes the shaman in you.

# CONCLUSION

If you have made it this far, you have officially completed all of the steps to becoming a shadow worker. I welcome you to read and reread this book whenever you wish, as it will continue to work for different parts of the shadow to come forward. I have been doing personal shadow work for decades now, and there still are pieces of my shadow that decide when I am ready for them to emerge. Self-discovery is a never-ending process, and so it is with the shadow side too.

Feel free to add elements or tools from this book to your own personal healing processes—this is not an all-or-nothing method. If you are a healer, feel free to apply any and/or all of these steps to your modalities. Moving through this book and its four main steps has granted you the rite of passage into shadow work. Only once we have healed ourselves can we assist another in healing themselves.

As I wrote this book, I had to engage my shadow. I began to wonder what kind of a world I would live in if I was able to express my complete self, including my shadow. How many more individuals would relate to my experiences? Moreover, how much more comfortable would I be with myself? My shadow self respected the time and energy of this work and needed to tell me a little bit more about myself. My shadow self once again invited me to connect with my complete self, not to disengage or run from it. Rather, my shadow wanted me to continue my deep self-love journey, which includes shadow work. Once again, I understand more of who I am, as well as the experiences that I have lived through to become my authentic self. I could view my life from the position of the victim; I could view my life from a controlling, defensive stance. However, I choose to view my life as an opportunity to learn and grow into my authentic self and to share this love and acceptance with others.

This work is not for the faint of heart. This work is for individuals who seek to understand how they arrived at their perspective and position. I wish the people around me understood why I am the way that I am, but in truth, it is not their job. It is my job to understand myself and to share my true, authentic self with others.

What happens when we deny our shadow? If I deny my shadow, I am denying parts of myself. I am rejecting aspects of myself. If I am rejecting myself, where will I seek acceptance? I will seek acceptance from outside sources. I will become who others tell me I should be, and I will lose my inner compass and my inner voice. At that point, I am opening myself up to being blindly led without considering if I am being authentic. I will lose myself and am only what society tells me is acceptable. Although this might not sound too harmful, as I sit with this idea of being blindly led without my inner compass, I see how easy it would be to fall into harm's way.

When we approach, recognize, understand, and respect the shadow, we promote self-acceptance. Self-acceptance includes all aspects of self, which gives me the liberty to heal, mature, and support my personal development. I no longer depend solely on others' acceptance, as I have acceptance within. I become more self-aware without feeling trapped in shame and blame. I have the ability to be myself and continue to progress in life. Additionally, when I come to terms with my shadow, it is easier to accept others.

Do we call forth the shadow, or does the shadow ask us to be present? Well, does the moon call the wolf, or does the wolf call the moon? The truth is that both are simultaneously happening. The shadow is not some devilish expression of a lower vibration of who and what we are; the shadow is organic, yet is an aspect of self that frightens some. If you have made it this far, I know that your shadow has called to you.

Maybe your shadow has called to you in order for you to expand your own thoughts about who and what you are. Maybe your shadow has called to you because you are ready for more of the truths that you were not necessarily able to handle before now. The shadow is not to be feared; the shadow wanted to protect you from the hard truths of life and the reality that you were not able to understand. Maybe it is time to grow and embrace what your shadow wants to share with you. It is time to have a final one-on-one conversation with the shadow.

## THE FINAL CONVERSATION WITH THE SHADOW

Although I am calling this section the final conversation with the shadow, my hope is that this is one of many conversations that you will have with your shadow. Take a moment to relax.

*I invite you to breathe. Breathe in this place. Remember the entire journey that you just embarked upon. You began in the morning, in a prairie. You spotted the ravens and recognized the pyre, the sacrificial mound. What were you going to sacrifice, or whose death did you need to witness? The answer is that you stood before the pyre and the death of old ways of understanding. You said farewell to the idea that you did not have a shadow or that the shadow was too scary to get to know, let alone understand and respect—even love. Although you might not have realized it, your shadow stood right behind you in the morning light, also facing the pyre. Your shadow was with you the whole time. Your shadow understood that being here was going to change the relationship between the two of you. The death of the old ways of understanding came as a relief to your shadow, as it was going to be recognized. Take time to reflect on what you journaled after this Ingress and Portal. Your shadow wrote some of this to provide you with clues that would reunite the two of you.*

*I invite you to breathe. Breathe in this place. You moved into the arroyo, the heat of the sun, and the dryness of the desert. You spotted the snake, and its spirit helped you understand how your shadow devel-*

*oped. Your shadow was supporting you in this experience—you just couldn't see it because it was noontime, and it was positioned beneath your feet, holding you up. At this point, you began to shake off old energy and thoughts of what your shadow is or was. Your shadow was with you in this experience. Your shadow began to feel that you wanted to understand your past, and not only from the perspective that was comfortable for your light side. You were ready for the fuller truth of the darkness that was hard for your light side to understand—the truth your shadow had carried all along. Again, reflect on what you wrote in your journal after this Ingress and Portal. Your shadow began to reveal its truths to you here.*

*I invite you to breathe. Breathe in this place. You were in a moist landscape, a landscape where you felt safe enough to express yourself and your emotions a little bit more. You were in a place where you began to relax and understand the emotional impact of everything you had been through and everything you had dealt with. You found a crystal, a tool that assisted you in understanding what it was that you were seeking. Up until this point, you thought you were merely seeking the shadow, and possibly the wisdom of the shadow. But in this moment, your shadow was able to gently reach out to you and provide you with understanding via the crystal it left for you to find. This crystal was a message from your shadow. Please reflect on what you wrote in your journal—your shadow was with you the whole time.*

*I invite you to breathe. Breathe in this place. You found yourself in a moonlit forest. A feeling of solitude may have washed over you for a moment or two. However, you also had the sensation that something was watching you. Your shadow was there, awaiting you, wondering if you would be willing to release your connection to your old understandings of self. Wondering if you would realize where you came from. Wondering if you would take the journey to discover it. Wondering if it could leave you messages via crystals along the way. Wondering if you would make it to the forest. Your shadow led you here. Feel free to reflect on your journal prompts—your shadow was with you the whole time.*

*We're All One. I am your shadow and I have been watching over you your entire life. I have spoken up when you felt you didn't have a voice. I have defended you against threatening situations when you were simply hoping for the best. I have given warnings to those who may want to hurt you. I have led you here to reconnect with you. I am so happy that you now recognize me; you know more of my origin. You are beginning to understand me and respect me. I recognize you, know your story, understand you, and respect you—I love you. I have watched over you. I am you. Thank you for finding me!*

*With Love,*
*Your Shadow*

# APPENDIX
# VISUALIZATION BASICS

Visualization may or may not come naturally. In this book, I have asked you to visualize in your mind's eye during the Ingress and Portal guided meditations. Everyone perceives in slightly different ways; I focus on the five senses: sight, smell, touch, taste, and sound. Each of these senses helps us understand the environment. It is the same when it comes to embarking on a guided meditation—the only difference is that in a guided meditation, we use the five senses to perceive the inner world. Just as in life, some senses might be stronger than others. Here is a quick exercise for you to explore your personal strengths and opportunities for development.

*Take a few deep breaths and find a relaxed position. Imagine that you are standing in*

*front of a closed door that leads to a beautiful land-scape. Take a moment, and when you are ready, gently open the door and step into the landscape. Allow the landscape to settle in place. As you move into the landscape, a bird flies above your head.*

1. Did you see the bird?
2. Did you hear the bird?
3. Or did you simply know that it was there, without seeing the bird?

*You continue to move into the landscape. In the distance, there is a tree. Imagine that you are moving toward the tree, and you see a picnic basket on a table underneath the tree. Go to the picnic basket and open it up. Inside is a ripe orange. Begin to peel the orange.*

4. Can you feel the weight of the orange?
5. Can you smell the orange?
6. Or do you simply know these things without additional sensations?

*You grab a slice of the orange and take a bite.*

7. Did you taste the orange?
8. Did your mouth begin to salivate?
9. Or are you simply aware of this experience without any additional sensations?

*Look around at the landscape.*

10. How do you perceive it?

11. Are there any additional imaginings within the landscape that have not been mentioned yet? If so, note your perceptions.

> *Now it is time to return to the door. When you are ready, step back through the doorway and allow the door to gently close behind you. Return your consciousness to the space and time you are physically in. If needed, wiggle your fingers and toes.*

Which one of your senses was most active? It's possible that you simply knew things without additional sensations, which is fine too. Give yourself permission to imagine in the way that you naturally do.

If you want to increase your visualization ability, here is one more technique to assist you: I invite you to imagine that you are holding something in your hands. Ask yourself the following questions, and take your time with the answers.

1. What size is it?

2. How much does it weigh?

3. Does it have a color?

4. What does it look like?

5. Is there anything else that you notice?

Practicing visualization and taking the time to understand how you perceive things will strengthen the way that you perceive your inner world.

# BIBLIOGRAPHY

Bohm, David. *On Dialogue*. Routledge, 2004.

Campbell, Joseph. *The Hero with a Thousand Faces*. New World Library, 2008.

Freud, Sigmund. "The Ego and the Id (1923)." *TACD Journal* 17, no. 1 (1989): 5–22. https://doi.org/10.1080/1046171X.1989.12034344.

Gibran, Kahlil. *The Prophet*. Alfred A. Knopf, 1923. Google Books.

Goldberg, Simon B., Brian T. Pace, Christopher R. Nicholas, Charles L. Raison, and Paul R. Hutson. "The Experimental Effects of Psilocybin on Symptoms of Anxiety and Depression: A Meta-Analysis." *Psychiatry Research* 284 (2020). https://doi.org/10.1016/j.psychres.2020.112749.

Hall, Judy. *The Encyclopedia of Crystals*. Fair Winds Press, 2006.

Judith, Anodea. *Wheels of Life: A User's Guide to the Chakra System*. Llewellyn Publications, 2021.

Jung, C. G. *Mysterium Coniunctionis: An Inquiry into the Separation and Synthesis of Psychic Opposites in Alchemy*. Vol. 14 of *The Collected Works of C. G. Jung*, edited by Sir Herbert Read, Michael Fordham, and Gerhard Adler. Routledge, 2014. Google Books.

———. *Part I: Archetypes and the Collective Unconscious*. Vol. 9 of *The Collected Works of C. G. Jung*, edited and translated by Gerhard Adler and R. F. C. Hull. Princeton University Press, 1990. Google Books.

Levine, Peter A. *Waking the Tiger: Healing Trauma*. With Ann Frederick. North Atlantic Books, 2023.

Mcleod, Saul. "Erik Erikson's Stages of Psychological Development." SimplyPsychology. Updated January 25, 2024. https://www.simplypsychology.org/erik-erikson.html.

Nietzsche, Friedrich. *Beyond Good & Evil: Prelude to a Philosophy of the Future*. Edited and translated by Walter Kaufmann. Vintage Books, 1989. Google Books.

———. *On the Genealogy of Morals and Ecce Homo*. Edited by Walter Kaufmann. Translated by Walter Kaufmann and R. J. Hollingdale. Vintage Books, 1989. Google Books.

Peck, M. Scott. *The Road Less Traveled: A New Psychology of Love, Traditional Values, and Spiritual Growth*. Simon & Schuster, 1985.

Prior, Helmut, Ariane Schwarz, and Onur Güntürkün. "Mirror-Induced Behavior in the Magpie (Pica Pica): Evidence of Self-Recognition." *PLOS Biology* 6, no. 8 (2008). https://doi.org/10.1371/journal.pbio.0060202.

Reber, Arthur S. *The Penguin Dictionary of Psychology*. Penguin Books, 1985.

Ruffell, Simon G. D., Max Crosland-Wood, Rob Palmer, Nige Netzband, WaiFung Tsang, Brandon Weiss, Sam Gandy, Tessa Cowley-Court, Andreas Halman, Diana McHerron, Angelina Jong, Tom Kennedy, Eleanor White, Daniel Perkins, Devin B. Terhune, and Jerome Sarris. "Ayahuasca: A Review of Historical, Pharmacological, and Therapeutic Aspects." *PCN Reports* 2, no. 4 (2023). https://doi.org/10.1002/pcn5.146.

Whitcomb, Bill. *The Magician's Companion: A Practical & Encyclopedic Guide to Magical & Religious Symbolism*. Llewellyn Publications, 1993.

Wilson, Robert, Jr. "The Caduceus and Its Symbolism." *Annals of Medical History* 4, no. 3 (1922): 301–3. https://www.ncbi.nlm.nih.gov/pmc/articles/PMC7034607.

Xavier, Gregory, Anselm Su Ting, and Norsiah Fauzan. "Exploratory Study of Brain Waves and Corresponding Brain Regions of Fatigue On-Call Doctors Using Quantitative Electroencephalogram." *Journal of Occupational Health* 62, no. 1 (Jan./Dec. 2020). https://doi.org/10.1002/1348-9585.12121.

## TO WRITE TO THE AUTHOR

If you wish to contact the author or would like more information about this book, please write to the author in care of Llewellyn Worldwide Ltd. and we will forward your request. Both the author and publisher appreciate hearing from you and learning of your enjoyment of this book and how it has helped you. Llewellyn Worldwide Ltd. cannot guarantee that every letter written to the author can be answered, but all will be forwarded. Please write to:

Granddaughter Crow
⅟ Llewellyn Worldwide
2143 Wooddale Drive
Woodbury, MN 55125-2989

Please enclose a self-addressed stamped envelope for reply,
or $1.00 to cover costs. If outside the U.S.A., enclose
an international postal reply coupon.

Many of Llewellyn's authors have websites with additional information and resources. For more information, please visit our website at http://www.llewellyn.com.